THE TROUBADOURS AND ENGLAND

CAMBRIDGE UNIVERSITY PRESS
C. F. CLAY, Manager
LONDON : FETTER LANE, E.C. 4

NEW YORK : THE MACMILLAN CO.
BOMBAY, CALCUTTA, MADRAS } MACMILLAN & CO., LTD.
TORONTO : THE MACMILLAN CO. OF CANADA, LTD.
TOKYO : MARUZEN-KABUSHIKI-KAISHA

THE TROUBADOURS
AND
ENGLAND

BY

H. J. CHAYTOR, M.A.
FELLOW OF ST CATHARINE'S COLLEGE, CAMBRIDGE

CAMBRIDGE
AT THE UNIVERSITY PRESS
1923

PRINTED IN GREAT BRITAIN

PREFACE

MANY histories of literature which deal with the Middle English lyric refer in more or less vague and general terms to the influence exerted by the Provençal troubadours upon this part of our national poetry; no one, so far as I know, has yet attempted to estimate the full extent of this influence or to trace the manner in which it was exerted. This book is an attempt to fill the gap. The foreign element in Middle English poetry has been touched upon by O. Heider, *Untersuchungen zur mittelenglischen erotischen Lyrik*, Inaugural-Dissertation zur Erlangung der Doctorwürde, Halle, 1906, a treatise of little value. Some useful information, of which I have availed myself, is to be found in A. Brandl, "Spielmannsverhältnisse in frühmittelenglischer Zeit," *Sitzungsberichte der königlich preussischen Akademie der Wissenschaften*, 1910. *Les Troubadours et l'Angleterre*, Jean Audiau, Tulle, 1920, is a thesis submitted to the Faculty of Letters at Toulouse for the Diplôme d'Études Supérieures de Langue Anglaise; the author refers to my observations on the subject in *The Troubadours*, Cambridge, 1912 (Cambridge Manuals of

Science and Literature), and I have to thank him for two references to unpublished MSS. The limits of his suggestive thesis did not allow him fully to develop the subject.

I have not attempted to estimate the influence of the troubadours upon Chaucer and Gower; in view of the many literary influences with which they were in contact, it seems doubtful whether any such estimate is possible. The subject is by no means exhausted: for instance, a comparison of troubadour melodies with those preserved in English MSS. might well throw further light upon the question, if any specialist in mediaeval music cared to undertake the task.

In the course of an enquiry which necessarily ranges over a wide field, errors of omission and of commission can doubtless be laid to my charge. I can only hope to have made the path a little easier for future investigators.

H. J. C.

St Catharine's College,
Cambridge.
December, 1922.

CONTENTS

I

THE CONDITIONS UNDER WHICH THE ENGLISH LYRIC WAS EVOLVED

THE professional entertainer was a feature of English social life long before the Norman Conquest. In 679, the church council held at Rome to deal with English affairs prohibited the clergy from maintaining "citharoedas[1]," and the council of Clovesho in 747 ordered "ut monasteria...non sint ludicrarum artium receptacula, hoc est poetarum, citharistarum, musicorum, scurrarum." This catalogue appears to distinguish poets who recited or sang their own compositions from minstrels who sang the compositions of others, and from clowns, tumblers and buffoons who used other devices for attracting and holding an audience. Miniatures of the 8th and 9th centuries show the native gleeman performing the same functions as the Latin mimus and designated as *mimus* and as *histrio*. Some of these may have been foreigners: Gutbereht, the abbot of Newcastle, wrote to a continental bishop asking him for a *citharoeda*. Generally speaking, the Church maintained an attitude of hostility to

[1] Haddan-Stubbs, *Councils*, III, 133 and 339, quoted by E. Faral, *Les Jongleurs en France au moyen âge*, Bibl. de l'école des hautes études, Fasc. 687, Paris, 1910. See also Alois Brandl, "Spielmannsverhältnisse in frühmittelenglischer Zeit," *Sitzungsberichte der königlich preuss. Akademie*, No. 41, 1910.

the minstrel and jongleur class in pre-Norman as well as in Norman times. Even so cultivated a man as John of Salisbury points out that patristic writings declared jongleurs to be excommunicated by their profession, and they are repeatedly described as the ministers of Satan, the corrupters of youth and the scum of humanity; they are classed with epileptics, magicians and prostitutes, and are without hope of salvation in this world or the next. Thus we can understand the horror of a bishop of Worcester, when one of his priests, according to Giraldus Cambrensis, inadvertently chanted at the altar, "Sweet lemman, thine ore," instead of "Dominus vobiscum." Thomas Becket, as chancellor, had shown hospitality and friendliness to minstrels; as archbishop, he forbade them his palace. This, the official attitude, was not always strictly maintained; at certain festivals in England, the minstrels of great lords were allowed to practise their art as they pleased: in 1441, the Priory of Maxtoke paid four shillings to Lord Clinton's minstrels, and only two to the officiating priests[1].

The Church, while discouraging secular minstrelsy, was quite aware of the importance of music and song, if only for liturgical purposes. The love of Grosteste, bishop of Lincoln, for music and his domestic harper, is a well-known case, and by no means unusual. Nigellus Wireker says of the raising of William de Longchamp, bishop of Ely, to the chancellorship in 1190: "quidam carmina,

[1] Faral, p. 30. See Chambers, *Mediaeval Stage*, II, append. E. Cloetta, *Poème moral*, ad fin.

quidam cantilenas et alias hujusmodi, quae non multo constabant, magnifice offerebant, ut ubertate frugum alterius seminum suorum inopiam sublevarent[1]." The domestic accounts of Bishop Swinfield of Hereford for the year 1289–90 show payments "cithoeristae domini Abbatis Radingi," "Benetto violatori," a player on the viol, and to other minstrels and jugglers (menestrallis et wafferariis). Two country minstrels who performed before the bishop at Monkton on the occasion of his visitation received a penny each, considerably less than was paid to the more accomplished artistes mentioned above[2].

Thus professional minstrels succeeded even in entering churches to reinforce the choir or to give special performances. The clerks errant, the "vagrants," who wandered about the country included men who had been trained as minstrels, and if their disorderly life produced the special class known as Goliards, there is evidence on the other hand that some of them did the work of the Church in singing religious poems, hymns, and reciting the lives of the Saints[3].

But to the general and persistent hostility of the Church is due the comparative scarcity of reference to vernacular poetry[4]. The Church produced most

[1] Rolls Series. Anglo-Latin satirical poets, I, 215.

[2] Camden Society, 1853, pp. 147, 152.

[3] Thomas Cabham, *Poenitentia*. "Sunt...qui dicuntur joculatores, qui cantant gesta principum et vitas sanctorum. Bene possunt sustineri tales." Faral, p. 44.

[4] Wistan, bishop of Worcester in 1062, is reported by William of Malmesbury (*Gesta Pontificum*, Rolls Series, p. 281) to have had

of the historical writing of the age and certainly influenced the attitude of writers who were not themselves ecclesiastics. It is not too much to say that indifference or contempt on the part of a writer with reference to minstrels is adequate evidence of his ecclesiastical profession. Many such writers were cultivated men, as the times went, and their works are often bespattered with quotations from Latin classical authors: but casual and contemptuous references to "joculatores et histriones" mark the extent of their interest in the current poetry of their times; many also produced a large amount of inferior Latin elegiacs and hexameters by efforts which might from our point of view have been more profitably expended upon composition in their own language. Peter of Peckham begins his life of St Richard[1], written 1267–8, with a declaration that secular poems are waste of time and worse.

> Si l'un cunte romanz d'amur,
> k'en vient del oïr a chief de tur?
> Ne sai, for mettre le penser
> en folie, folement amer;
> e quel profit (en) vient de cunter
> de la pruesce un chevalier
> for sulement le delit del oïr,
> ke suvent (les) autres fet esbaudir?
> Mes icel esbaudissement
> de orgoil vient veraiement
> que contraire est a humilité
> ke veie nus dune a sauveté.

a fair knowledge of literature "praeter fabulas poetarum...quae nec nosset neque nosse dignaretur."

[1] Ed. A. T. Baker, *Revue des langues romanes*, 1910.

Robert Mannyng in the first lines of his *Handlyng Synne* speaks of the prevailing taste "that talys and rymys wyl blethly here" which lead to sin, and writes to provide something better than "al swych foul manere." The strictures in *Piers Plowman* are directed rather against the patrons than the minstrels.

Thus there was an opposition between the Church and the minstrel class which is represented in the well-known *Owl and Nightingale*; the secular nobility did not share the prejudices of the Church and in some cases professional minstrels were drawn from their class. The 14th century English version of Tristan (Sir Tristrem) makes much of the hero's attainments as a minstrel: his gift of song enables him to attract the fair Ysonde; he earns money by his talent; when a rival harper with a finer instrument has enticed Ysonde away, Tristrem wins her back by his own skill, and the English adapter of the story has laid special emphasis upon this *motif*.

Thus the persistent hostility of the Church is evidence enough to show that the taste for minstrelsy was deeply rooted in English society. The Norman Conquest had greatly changed the position and prospects of the English *scôp* and *gleeman*, but the nature and process of the change remain obscure. The society entertainers whom the Normans and their successors brought with them would obviously hold the more distinguished positions; the native singers might either learn a new technique from the invaders or might continue with stubborn patriotism to declaim the old songs to such audiences as they could find. So far as they depended for a livelihood upon their art, theirs was clearly a losing position and eventually the only members of the craft who remained were such as consented to recognise foreign taste and foreign technique. Ten Brink believed that the English singer, the Anglo-Saxon *scôp*, remained throughout the Norman period a class distinct from the French minstrel; if he was driven out of sight by new political and social conditions after the Conquest, he none the less retained a certain popularity among the conquered, and the battle poems of Laurence Minot about the middle of the 14th century may be taken as evidence for a temporary revival of native art: not until Chaucer's time and because of his influence did this class entirely disappear. But Ten Brink admitted that the native *scôp* could not entirely escape foreign influences, and such evidence as there is seems to show that the English singers did not long maintain their exclusiveness. No direct connection between the professions of *jongleur* and *scôp* can be shown; it can only be stated that the demand for their public performances was permanent and widespread and that they were valued not only as entertainers, but as newsmongers.

The growth of French influence upon poetry is shown by the number of new terms describing the poet's profession which came into use after the outset of the 12th century. The English *scôp* had been a singer and if he combined with this art other tricks of entertainment, tumbling, juggling or the like, he was a *gleeman*. The term *scôp* is replaced by *harpour*, *sautreour*, *rymour*, also by *disour*, and *gestour* for narrative poets. Both *scôp* and *gleeman* were *minstrels*, or in Latin *mimi*, *histriones*, *joculatores*. The mere variety artist was a *japer*, *jangler*, *juglour* or *tregetour*[1]. *Goliardeis* was in the first instance a special kind of clerical satirist. Of these, *minstrel* becomes the most general term.

The obviously unhistorical story of King Alfred's entry into the Danish camp in the disguise of a minstrel is repeated with variations from the 12th to the 14th century. Olaf, the Viking king, entered Athelstan's camp at Brunanburg in a similar manner. The story reappears in Geoffrey of Monmouth's *Historia Britonum*, where Baldulf, disguised as a minstrel, is able to pass through the army besieging York and to reach his brother who was shut up in the town. In *King Horn*, entrance is gained to a castle by the hero as a harper when all others are refused admission[2]. Such incidents are only possible if the minstrel had a definite position in society, was a wanderer from place to place and welcome wherever he went.

After 1150 the terms jongleur and trouvère (or better, trouveur) appear in England. Theoretically and in practice in Provence itself, the trouveur was a composer of lyric poems and the jongleur the performer of them. But even during the classical period of Provençal lyric poetry, one and the same

[1] Chaucer's term.
[2] Other cases in Brandl, *op. cit.* p. 884.

man might be joglar and trobador; and in northern France and England the distinction was almost without meaning. Both terms may denote one man as composer or performer, though a jongleur implied a man who gave any kind of public entertainment, from singing hymns to the Virgin to tumbling or juggling. The well-known passage in Thomas Cabham's *Penitential* (end of the 13th century) is not conclusive, as he was chiefly concerned to decide which classes of performers were "damnabiles" and which might be tolerated. Nor are attempts to distinguish between a *jonglerie seignurale*, descended from the Anglo-Saxon bards, and a *jonglerie foraine* any more successful[1]. The jongleur attached to a court was undoubtedly in a better position[2] and in a more refined atmosphere than the wandering entertainer. But the aristocrat was ready to descend to lower and grosser levels, if he saw no other means of earning his bread. Under such circumstances he was equally willing to recite a chanson de geste or to exhibit a performing monkey. In both cases the object was reward. The street singer exhorted his patrons to be generous and made his collection; the jongleur at a nobleman's court expected gifts of money, furs, horses, jewels and sometimes obtained even more. Berdic, the minstrel of William the Conqueror, possessed three "villas" in the county of Gloucester; Richard

[1] Chambers, *Mediaeval Stage*, I, 63. The evidence is fully discussed by Faral, p. 80.

[2] Henry II (Household ordinances, 48) treated minstrels and heralds as equal.

Jeffrey, court minstrel to Henry V and Henry VI, held the district of Vaux-sur-Mer in Normandy. The English exchequer rolls show considerable sums expended in this way during the 13th and 14th centuries[1]; and the knighting of Prince Edward in 1306 at Whitsuntide (a favourite festival for jongleur performances) was an occasion of great extravagance. Employers sometimes used their jongleurs as messengers in affairs where tact and discretion were required. When Edward II was keeping Whitsuntide at Westminster in 1317, a chronicler[2] states that "quaedam mulier ornatu histrionali redimita, equum bonum, histrionaliter phaleratum, ascensa, dictam aulam intravit, mensas more histrionum circumivit, ad descum per gradus ascendit, mensae regiae audacter appropinquavit, quandam literam coram rege posuit, et, retracto freno, salutatis hospitibus, absque strepitu vel impedimento eques discessit," whence it would appear that women might also follow the profession, as in Provence. In 1383, an English knight, going to France to fight with Guy de la Trémoille, took his jongleurs with him at a cost of 100 *livres d'or*. In 1415, Henry V of England engaged eighteen minstrels to follow him to Guienne and elsewhere[3].

[1] Chambers, *Mediaeval Stage*, II, 234.

[2] Jean de Trokelove, *Annales* (Rerum brit. script. p. 38) quoted by Faral, p. 114.

[3] Faral quotes the contract from Rymer, *Foedera*, "Ceste endenture, faite le v jour de juijn, l'an tierce nostre sovereigne seigneur le roi Henri, puis le conquest quint, tesmoigne que John Clyff, ministral, et autres XVII ministralls, ount receuz de nostre dit seigneur le roy, par le mayns de Thomas count d'Arundel et de Surrie, tresorer d'Engleterre, xi l.s sur lour gages a chescun de ceux xii d le jour,

Minstrels were also engaged for purposes other than entertainment. Bishop Longchamp, the chancellor of Richard Cœur de Lion, during the king's absence, hired them to sing his praises in public[1]. A clever jongleur could make or mar a reputation: in the *Ancren Riwle*, Flatterer and Backbiter are represented as two *menestrans*. Henry I threatened to put out the eyes of the captured minstrel Luc de la Barre for composing *estrabots* satirising the throne[2]. A statute of Sarum warns churchpeople against minstrels with their *laude*, *immo verius fraude* and their *detractationibus*. They were employed also as historians: Wace wrote for Henry II of England, and Geoffroi Gaimar wrote his *Histoire des Anglais* for Constance, wife of Robert Fiz-Gislebert. In these respects the jongleur becomes more than a mere entertainer.

Jongleurs produced epics, romans d'aventure, fabliaux, lais and undoubtedly much lyric poetry. In the *Deux bourdeurs ribauds*, one of them declares (II, 148),

> Si sei porter consels d'amors,
> Et faire chapelez de flors,
> Et çainture de druerie
> Et beau parler de cortoisie
> A ceus qui d'amors sont espris.

pur demy quarter de l'an, pur servir nostre dit seigneur le roy es parties de Guyen, ou aillours..." etc.

[1] Roger of Hoveden, *Chronicon* (Rerum brit. script. III, 143), "hic ad augmentum et famam sui nominis emendicata carmina et rhythmos adulatorios comparabat et de regno Francorum cantores et joculatores muneribus allexerat, ut de illo canerent in plateis et jam dicebatur ubique, quod non erat talis in orbe."

[2] Ordericus Vitalis, *Hist. Eccles.* II, 19.

To this catalogue, religious poetry must be added, much of which was in Latin, but even the Latin lyrics show traces of Provençal influence, both in form and spirit. Thomas of Bayeux, archbishop of York, is said by William of Malmesbury to have adapted secular songs for religious purposes: "si quis in audita ejus arte joculatoria aliquid vocale sonaret, statim illud in divinas laudes effigiare[1]"; these adaptations were probably Latin hymns to the Virgin.

French culture was readily accepted as soon as the Conquest had become an accomplished fact and the French language soon made its way into almost every class of society. It became the legal language as early as the time of Henry I; it was usual in the pulpit in the reign of Richard I, and as it was then used in the baronial courts, it was presumably understood by the tenant class. French was also the language of commerce by sea and land; the records of the merchant guilds of the 13th and 14th centuries are almost entirely in French. The famous sea-laws of Oléron, the chief and generally accepted navigation acts of the time, were in French, and no Latin version of them appears to have existed, nor was any English translation made until the 16th century. These facts presuppose a widespread knowledge of French.

The oldest extant version of the ordinances by which the Guild merchant first, and later also the borough (of Southampton) were governed, is in Norman-French, and there is no reason to suppose that they were originally

[1] *Gesta Pontificum*, Rolls Series, p. 258.

drawn up in another language, even though some of them may represent Anglo-Saxon customs. These ordinances had to be read and discussed at Guild meetings, new members had to promise to obey them; nevertheless, no English translation of them was made till 1473. Yet the persons admitted into the Guild were not scholars, but merchants and artisans. If French had not been perfectly familiar to them, they would at least have taken the oath in English[1].

By the end of the 13th century French had become the fashionable language in all classes of society.

While Latin and French were thus the two "cultural" languages, trilingualism was more common than is often supposed. In so remote a district as southern Cornwall a bishop's visitation in 1356 was conducted in three languages, English, French and Cornish[2]. Raoul de Tremur, a heretic, excommunicated in 1355–6 was *lingua quadruplici latina, gallica, anglica et cornabecaque et britannica garrulus et disertus*. Bishop Longchamp's performers sang to the common people, and must have used the English vernacular if they appealed to the lowest classes; even if the story be a slander circulated by the bishop's enemies, it must have been a possibility or it would not have gained credence. Songs of this period exist composed in English with a refrain in French or Latin: the special Anglo-Norman dialect was, in part, the result of attempts by Englishmen to speak French and the metrical peculiarities of

[1] P. Studer, *The Oak Book of Southampton*, Southampton, 1911, Supplement, p. 8.

[2] J. Loth, *Contribution à l'étude des romans de la Table Ronde*, Paris, 1912, p. 71.

Anglo-Norman verse are, generally speaking, caused by attempts to combine the Teutonic stress system with the Romance syllabic system of metre. Thus, while Englishmen learned French, Frenchmen learned English. Of the numerous minstrels who came to the court in London when Edward II was knighted in 1306, many seem to have been Frenchmen who adopted English names for the time being; some of them wandered about the country after the festivities, visiting Norman castles and also picking up a living wherever they could find an audience. They became such a nuisance that legislation was required to limit their movements. Such performers must have used French and English with equal readiness, according to the nature of the audiences which they entertained. French was spoken in England before the Norman Conquest, though only by the few foreigners who had special reasons for settling in England: the favourites, for instance, brought over by Edward the Confessor. After the Conquest, French was the official language and was spoken in all those circles where any literary works were likely to gain a hearing. Two hundred years elapsed before a King of England used English as his mother tongue. In 1363 English was first used in the speech in which the chancellor opened Parliament. English was not heard in the law-courts before the time of Henry III. On the other hand, the Norman conquerors made no attempt to suppress or to extirpate the English language: until the loss of Normandy in 1204, the need of a language common to islanders and continentals maintained the value of French; when John and Philippe Auguste agreed that no vassal should hold lands both in England and Normandy, French became a foreign language, though it continued in use for a long time. In the 13th century a knowledge of French was deemed a necessary accomplishment for anyone who wished to rise in the world: "for but a man knows French, he is esteemed but little," said Robert of Gloucester. Robert Mannyng begins his *Handlyng Synne* in 1303 by saying that he writes in English for the benefit of the uneducated,

For lewde men y undyrtoke
On englyssh tunge to make thys boke.

The middle classes demanded and obtained opportunities of learning French; it was the medium of instruction in grammar schools and when one John of Cornwall taught in English in 1345, he doubtless made a remarkable innovation. Towards the end of the 13th century Gautier de Bibbysworth wrote an elementary treatise for the benefit of children who wished to learn French. One of the most interesting of the treatises which followed this work is *La manière de Langage*[1] written in 1396, which is the first example of a conversation book for the use of foreigners. The author had travelled in France and attempts to reproduce conversations suitable to different classes of society: he inserts fragments of songs on five occasions, a fact which shows the popularity of these compositions in his

[1] P. Meyer, *Revue critique d'histoire et de littérature*, 1870.

time: moreover, he apparently quotes from memory; one such fragment reproduces a troubadour commonplace,

> Tres doulz regart amerousement trait
> Tant de doulceur fait en mon cuer entrer
> Quant les miens yeulx te pevent racontrer
> Que tout mon sang me fuit et vers toi trait.

Thus French was widely spoken by numbers of people to whom it had never been a mother tongue, and who were in consequence able to appreciate continental poetry, lyric or narrative.

Robert Mannyng of Brunne, who wrote his *Handlyng Synne* in 1303, produced a translation of Peter Langtoft's chronicle about 1340. His prologue to this work contains a passage (which has been several times quoted) of importance for its bearing upon the position of English in his time. He says that he is writing for simple men, who do not know "strange English" and not for "disours, seggers (reciters) or harpours"; hence, for the benefit of the "lewed menn," he will avoid composing "in ryme couwee or in strangere or enterlace" and will use a simple metre. The transformations that other tales have undergone at the hands of reciters, translators and adaptors are an argument in favour of his method,

> I see in song, in sedgeying tale
> Of Erceldoun and of Kendale
> Non tham says as thai tham wroght,
> And in ther saying it semes noght.
> That may thou here in Sir Tristem;
> Ouer gestes it has the steem

Ouer alle that is or was
If menn it sayd as made Thomas.
Bot I here it no mann so say.

In other words, "the tales of Thomas of Erceldoun do not reproduce the work of the authors ('thai') from whom they are taken. The charm of the story disappears. Thomas of Erceldoun's Sir Tristem is a case in point. The story is esteemed above all narrative poems and deservedly so, if men would repeat it as Thomas, the Anglo-Norman poet, wrote it. But they do not."

Robert's criticism is sound: the story is cut down by Thomas of Erceldoun to about 3500 lines of complicated alliteration, whereas the remains of the version by the Anglo-Norman Thomas show him to have been a real poet. Robert proceeds to explain the cause of this difference,

Thai sayd it for pride and nobleye
That non were suylk as thei;
. . . .
Thai sayd in so quante Inglis
That manyone wate not what it is
Therfore I heuyed (*hesitated*) wele the more
In strange ryme to trauayle sore;
And my witte was oure thynne
So strange speche to trauayle in,
And forsoth I couthe noght
So strange Inglis as thai wroght
And menn besoght me many a tyme
To turn it bot in lighte ryme.

Robert thus contemplates the needs of three classes of readers: those who understood Anglo-Norman, those who preferred an elaborate and artificial diction of English, and those who required a plain tale simply told. The situation as regards

English was thus analogous to the opposition between the *trobar clus* and the *trobar plan* in southern France; the "strange ryme, strange speche and strange Inglis" appealed to a more cultivated and aristocratic class than that for which he himself was writing.

An enquiry into the origins of the Middle-English lyric must therefore consider the Anglo-Norman lyric which was produced during the same period. Poets may have composed in both languages: pieces remain, not always to be dignified by the name of poetry, in a mixture of English, Anglo-Norman and Latin, or in English and Anglo-Norman[1], which show, at any rate, much facility in passing from one language to another. There are religious as well as political examples of this device: e.g.

> Maiden, moder milde
> oïez cel oreysoun[2].

If Anglo-Norman influenced English, the reverse process can also be noted; certain Anglicisms imposed themselves upon the language and recur so frequently in Anglo-Norman literature that they must be considered to have there domesticated

[1] "Song of the Times," Wright, *Political Songs*, p. 251, in French, Latin and English. The editor might have printed it in half lines to show the rimes ab ab. This he has done in the song "On the King's breaking his Confirmation of Magna Charta" (p. 253) in French and English, from the Auchinleck MS. of Edinburgh. There is another version, as yet apparently not noted, of this poem in St John's College, Cambridge, MS. 112, f. 400 a, in Dr James' catalogue, which shows some interesting variations from the Edinburgh text.

[2] Böddeker, *Altenglische Dichtungen des MS. Harley* 2253, Berlin, 1878, p. 220.

themselves. *Comencer à* (to begin), with the infinitive, *faire* and the infinitive, are used as in the following,

> Tuz ses barons ad feit mander,
> La treson feit raconter,

which means simply "he has summoned his barons and relates the treachery," *faire* being suggested by the periphrastic form "he did relate." So *voleir* (*vouloir*) is constantly used to form a periphrastic future tense. *Entrer* is used with the accusative; so *mounter* (*monter*) un palefray, un destrier, etc. *Repeirer* is used in the sense of "to repair, betake oneself to a place." *Travailer* is used meaning "to travel." These and other syntactical and phonetic Anglicisms had become incorporated in Anglo-Norman before the close of the 14th century[1]. Thus, as connection with the Continent grew looser, Anglo-Norman assumed certain special characteristics which eventually were sufficiently pronounced to give it a dialectical character. It was a transplanted language with little or no possibility of organic growth, and decay was rapid. Writers had no environment by which they could, consciously or unconsciously, correct their speech, and simplifications—reductions of diphthongs and cases—occur in Anglo-Norman which anticipate similar processes in continental French. Writers were themselves conscious that Anglo-French was a

[1] *Studien zur englischen Philologie*, XXIV, 1906, "Über den Einfluss des Englischen auf das Anglonormannische," von E. Burghardt. Other evidence on the position of French in England is given in the introductory chapter to Miss Lambley's *The French Language in England*, Manchester Univ. Press, 1920.

debased idiom. A prologue to the life of St Edward the Confessor says (13th century)[1],

> Si joe l'ordre des cases ne gart,
> Ne ne juigne part a sa part;
> Certes nen dei estre reprise,
> Ke nel puis faire en nule guise.
> Qu'en Latin est nominatif
> Ço frai romanz acusatif.
> Un faus franceis sai d'Angletere
> Ke nel alai ailurs quere,
> Mais vus ki ailurs apris l'avez,
> La u mester iest, l'amendez.

The writer thus throws upon the reader the onus of correcting mistakes.

After 1350, English begins to reappear as a language used by the educated; in collections of correspondence, letters in English begin to replace letters in French[2]. If French had been necessary and fashionable, English had never been forgotten, and when changed political conditions isolated Anglo-Norman from the Continent, the revival was inevitable. An exposition of the Lord's Prayer, written in the second half of the 15th century, gives reasons for the use of English:

> Some can frenssh and no latyn
> That han vsed courtys and dwelled thereyn;
> And some can off latyn a party
> That can frenssh full febelly;
> And some vnderstondeth Englyssh
> That neyther kan latyn ne frenssh;

[1] A. T. Baker, *Mod. Lang. Review*, III, p. 374.

[2] *Recueil de Lettres anglo-françaises*, F. J. Tanquerey, Paris, 1916, p. xi.

But lered and lewed, olde and yonge,
All vnderstondyn Englyssh tonge[1].

Nor does the term Anglo-Norman refer exclusively to the dialect of the province of Normandy as used in England. William the Conqueror's army included men from all parts of France; after 1204, Normandy as a province was merged in the Ile-de-France, and at various times, as during the reign of Henry III, the court at least received infusions from southern France. The resultant of these converging influences was the English language as it appears in Chaucer's works: neither the language nor the spirit of his writings is a revival of English as it was before 1066; he is the product of the conditions which prevailed under Norman and Angevin government. The events which occurred under those governments profoundly modified both the English nation and its language, and these modifications were exhibited in literature. Some of them were due, mediately or immediately, to Provençal influence.

The extent to which Provençal influence is apparent in Middle-English lyric poetry will be seen later; but the question now arises whether this influence was directly exerted by such troubadours as visited England and by the taste of court circles for troubadour poetry, or whether it was transmitted through the medium of northern French lyrics. The evidence available does not justify any dogmatic answer; but while some influence may have been directly exerted by the troubadours them-

[1] Cambridge University Library MS. Ff. iv. 9.

selves there are also indications that the Provençal features which characterise many Middle-English lyrics were derived from the imitation of French and not of Provençal originals.

During the latter half of the 12th century the Provençal school in northern France began. Provençal influence is apparent in the form and content of poems, in direct imitation or translation of passages from the troubadours, and in the fact that Provençal poems are found in MS. collections of French lyrics. The courts of Eleanor, the wife of Henry II, and of her daughter, Marie of Champagne, appear to have been centres whence this influence spread. The fashion became especially current in Picardy, Champagne, Flanders and the Artois district and was in general confined to the aristocratic circles to whom it appealed: Conon de Bethune, Blondel de Nesle, Gace Brulé and the Châtelain de Coucy are well-known poets of this school in the 12th century. Thibaut IV, Count of Champagne and King of Navarre (1201–53), who shared in the Albigeois crusade and thus helped to destroy the school which he imitated, wrote crusade poems upon Provençal models. The greater part of this poetry repeats, in another language, the well-worn mannerisms of the troubadours: we find the usual introductory references to the spring or winter seasons, the sweet voice of the nightingale, the wounding glances of ladies' eyes, the tyranny of love, arranged with Provençal complications of stanza form and rime-distribution. The following instances will serve to show how the trick was done.

Bernart de Ventadorn's well-known poem *Non es meravelha* (Appel, no. 31) was popular in northern France and was imitated by Jacques d'Amiens, Eustache le Peintre, Vielart de Corbie and an anonymous poet,

> Ors ni leos non etz vos ges,
> que-m aucizatz, s'a vos me ren,

"You are neither a bear nor a lion to slay me if I yield to you," which Jacques d'Amiens thus reproduced:

> Mais j'ai grant tort, k'el ne m'ochirra mie:
> Ja n'est che pas ours, lions ne singlers.

The same troubadour's *Ab joi mou lo vers* (Appel, no. I, stanza vi) is imitated by Vielart de Corbie:

> Anc sa bela bocha rizens
> non cuidei, baizan me traïs,
> car ab un doutz baisar m'aucis,
> si ab autre no m'es guirens;
> c'atretal m'es per semblansa
> com de Peläus la lanza,
> que del seu colp no podi'om garir,
> si autra vetz no s'en fezes ferir,

"I never thought that her fair smiling mouth would betray me: for with a sweet kiss she kills me, if she does not heal me with another. It is to me in seeming, as the lance of Peleus, for from its stroke no one could be cured, unless he caused himself to be stricken with it a second time."

Thus the French poet:

> Las! por quoi me mis a l'essai
> De besier ma dame au vis cler?

La lance Pelee trouvai
El besier que je li donai,
Qui durement me fet grever,
Car se ne me repuis vanter
La endroit ou je me navrai,
Bien sai qu'a la mort avendrai[1].

Whatever may be the differences between Middle-English and Provençal lyric poetry, a similarity of form and of expression is unmistakable. Yet at the time when the English lyric, so far as is known, was developing, the troubadours were no more, and French lyric poetry was in a period of decadence. Hence we may conclude that it was from or through northern France that English poets acquired many tricks of the troubadour trade.

A further point will support this conclusion. Favourite Provençal poems could be and were translated into French without violent damage to their form or spirit: Richard's song in prison is an instance; a crusade song of Gaucelm Faidit[2] is in French in three manuscripts and the presumption is that the troubadour himself preferred this language to his own, probably because he was using a specially French form, the *rotruenge*[3]. Poems in this style were also written in Anglo-Norman and appear to derive directly from Provençal.

[1] Jeanroy, "Chansons françaises inédites," *Revue des langues romanes*, 1902. For *Peleus' Lance*, see Chaytor, *Troubadours of Dante*, p. 118, Oxford, 1902; it became a commonplace in love poems: see also Chaucer, *Squire's Tale*, 236 f.; Shakespeare, 2 *Henry VI*, Act v, Sc. i, l. 100.

[2] Crescini, *Canzone francese d'un trovatore provenzale*, Padua, 1910.

[3] See Appendix.

On the other hand, it is likely that many Englishmen were familiar with the Provençal language. It will be obvious that communication between England and central and southern France was frequent and continual, for purposes commercial and social, as well as military and political. While we may grant that northern French influence upon literature was preponderant until the end of John's reign, there is every reason to suppose a reversal in favour of southern influence after that date. When the loss of the northern provinces cut off communication with Gascony through the Channel ports, Bordeaux became more than ever the centre of intercourse; Henry III attempted to make it the governmental centre as the best point from which to oppose the French crown, and the port itself owed much of its development to English enterprise. Both countries felt that their association was to their mutual advantage; England provided a market for Gascon products and Gascony wanted English tin and wool; English rule was generally popular for the freedom and liberty which it allowed to the municipalities. If Henry III brought over Gascons as his wife's favourites, he also brought them in pursuance of a policy which was steadily followed by his son, that of training promising young foreigners at the English court and sending them home to govern in the English interest or retaining them in England as administrators. Edward's employment of Gascon officers in the Scottish wars was due rather to his imperialism than to his favouritism, a point of view which contemporary Englishmen were naturally unable to appreciate. Thus we find a Gascon, Guilhem de Tournemire, as controller of the royal mint in 1280; we find Gascon families settling in England and becoming naturalised[1]; one such, Edmond de Calhau, died as governor of Berwick-on-Tweed in 1376; we find merchants like Guilhem Servat of Cahors[2], a financier and shipowner, in relations with king, church and state; his activities extended from Norway to the Pyrenees, with London as their central point. These men cannot have left their own literature entirely at home.

In London, during the reigns of Henry III and Edward I, special privileges were repeatedly granted to foreign merchants; daily courts, similar to the *pie poudré* courts, were held for those of them whose business would not bear delay. We find Londoners dealing with merchants from Provence, Gascony and Bordeaux, from Catalonia and Navarre[3]. These were largely concerned with the importation of wine; wine of Provence and white wine of Gascony are particularly mentioned. Such few English words as are derived directly from Provençal are connected with shipping and the wine trade[4]. These

[1] Montagu Burrows, *The Family of Brocas of Beaurepaire*, London, 1886.

[2] *Vierteljahrschrift für Sozial- und Wirtschaftsgeschichte*, XI, 1913. F. Arenz, *Wilhelm Servat von Cahors als Kaufmann zu London 1273–1320*.

[3] Statute of Edward I, Feb. 1, regnal year 31, *Munimenta Gildhallae Londoniensis*, II, Part i, 205, Rolls Series.

[4] Colander or cullender (now a vegetable strainer, Prov. colador), funnel, puncheon, rack, spigot, league, noose. Skeat, *Mod. Lang. Review*, I, 285, II, 60. Chaucer's tregetour or juggler is a further

commercial relations obliged merchants to obtain a knowledge of Provençal, in which language shipping contracts might be drawn up. Thus, on December 15, 1305, an English merchant freighted certain cargo boats from Castelsarrasin to Bordeaux: "notum sit qu'En Guillelmes de Nordois, merchant d'Anglaterra, a afretat per carguar en las guabaras d'En P. Bartas et d'En Jorda de Vazus de Castel Sarrazi de lui methis Guilhelmes iiii tonels de vi etc."; the document proceeds to state the merchandise and to specify the risks of either party[1]. Equally important was the wine trade between Southampton and the south of France: the well-known Rolls of Oléron, which regulated the traffic, continually refer to Bordeaux as a starting point for this trade[2].

The history of the wine trade with the south of France[3] is of some importance, as the frequency and extent of this traffic brought continental ideas, as well as continental wines, to England. The trade first became of any magnitude in the reign of Henry II; before his time, and before the Norman Conquest, England had made wine from the produce of her own vineyards, but as soon as continental wines had obtained a footing in the country, the

instance. Seu = tallow (sebum), found in the Anglo-Norman records of Southampton, is a Provençal form: see P. Studer, *Mod. Lang. Review*, 1911, p. 182.

[1] *Ann. du Midi*, 26, year 1914, p. 84.

[2] P. Studer, *The Oak Book of Southampton*, Southampton, 1911, vol. II, p. xviii.

[3] *Histoire du Commerce et de la Navigation à Bordeaux*, F. Michel, Bordeaux, 1867.

native vineyards went out of cultivation. Idleness, the inclemency of the climate and the greater profit to be gained from grazing land, are suggested by contemporary writers as reasons for the abandonment of vine-culture; the plain fact was, as Peter of Blois declares, that English wine was horrible stuff, even at the king's court, and that no one would touch it who could get anything better; the growing cheapness of French wines and the increasing purchasing power of the English customer are enough to explain the decay of the English vineyard. King John granted privileges to the Bordeaux merchants and ran heavily into debt for wine obtained from the town of Bordeaux; Henry III paid his father's bills and himself imported largely; we find him also commissioning a Bordeaux merchant to purchase silken and other fabrics at Montpelier and elsewhere. It was, moreover, the exception for ships to make the crossing singly; the convoy system was generally adopted, and this implies a well-developed and organised trade. Merchants brought not only their wares and their foreign customs, but also their poetry.

About the end of the 13th century were drawn up in London for the festival of the Puy, the regulations which are preserved in considerable detail in the London Guildhall records[1]. The preamble is as follows:

[1] *Munimenta Gildhallae Londoniensis*, II, Part i, 216, Rolls Series; the punctuation might be improved and some of the readings seem dubious, but I have not made any change in those portions of the text quoted.

En le honur de Dieu, Madame Seinte Marie, touz Seinz, e toutes Seintes; e en le honour nostre Seignour le Roy e touz les Barons du pais; e por loial amour ensaucier. Et por ceo qe la ville de Lundres soit renomee de touz biens en tuz lieus; et por ceo qe jolietes, pais, honestez, douceur, deboneiretes, e bon amour, sanz infinite, soit maintenue. E pur ceo qe touz biens soient mis avaunt, e touz maus ariere.—Li amerous compaignoun qui sont demoraunt e repairaunt en la bone cite de Lundres ount ordinee, conferme, et establie une feste ke hom apele "Pui."

In spite of the use of Anglo-Norman French and the reference to the king and the barons, the "loving companions dwelling in and repairing to the good city of London" may very well have been in the first instance foreigners in want of some intellectual recreation, who were introducing an institution which they had known and valued abroad. The statutes, which are more detailed than any others of their kind, clearly show that they are a set of new regulations to improve the working of a pre-existing organisation; they limit, for instance, the amount to be expended upon the annual feast, which had become so extravagant an affair that some members had been obliged to resign in previous years. It is also stated that "tuit lui pluis de la compagnie sont marchauntz hauntaunz les feires," who were therefore unable to be in London upon the day previously appointed for the great feast, which was therefore transferred to the first Sunday after Trinity. The regulations prescribe the method for keeping and administering the property of the company, the contributions to be given by the members and the mode of electing the Prince; provision is also made for the completion of a chapel for religious observances and for masses for the souls of dead members. The primary purpose of the Puy was, however, to hear songs and to crown the best of them, on which point the regulations are as follows:

E por ceo qe la feste roiale du Pui est maintenue e establie principaument pur un chaunsoun reale corouner; de ci cum ele est par chansoun honore e enhaunsiee, sont tuit luy gentil compaignoun du Pui par dreite raisoun tenuz des chauncons roiaus avauncer a lur pouair, et especiaument cele qe est coroune par assent des compaignouns le jour de la graunt feste du Pui....Par quei il est ici purvu en droit de celes chauncons, qe chascun prince novel, le jour qil portera la coroune, et governera la feste du Pui, e si tost com il avera fait pendre son blasoun de ces armes en la sale ou la feste du Pui serra tenue, qe maintenaunt face atacher de souz son blazon la chauncoun qe estoit corounee le jour qil fut eslu novel prince, apertement et droitement escrite, saunz defaute. Kar nul chauntour par droit ne doit chauncoun reale chaunter, ne proffrir, a la feste du Pui, desqes a taunt qil veit la chauncoun corounee dreinement en lan prochainement passe devaunt honoure a son dreit, en le manere avauntdite.

E qe il ieit a les chauncouns juger eslu ii ou iii qi se conoisent en chaunt et en musike, pur les notes et les poinz del chaunt trier et examiner, auxi bien com la nature de la reson enditee. Kar saunz le chaunt ne doit om mie appeler une resoun endite chauncoun, ne chauncoun reale corounee ne doit estre saunz doucour de melodies chaunte.

The term "chaunsoun reale" may have been used in the technical sense of chant royal; but the insistence upon the equal importance of music and words is interesting, as it exactly reproduces troubadour theories upon the subject. The earliest Puy known to us is that in which the troubadour monk of Montaudon acted as judge: "e fo faitz seigner de la cort del Puoi Sta Maria, e de dar l'esparvier. Lonc temps ac la seignoria de la cort del Puoi, tro que la cortz se perdet[1]." This meeting was primarily intended as a tournament, and poetical competitions formed a subordinate part of it; it appears to have lasted for some years, as reference is made to it by other troubadours; and as Velay, the place of meeting, was in the possession of Robert I of Auvergne, a well-known patron of troubadours, he may well have been the founder of it. When northern France began to imitate troubadour lyric poetry and the taste for it had caught the bourgeois class, Puys were formed in many towns, Arras, Amiens, Rouen, Abbeville and others, retaining the name and dedication of the original institution. The London Puy was probably an imitation of one of these northern confraternities; the citizens of Amiens, Corbie and Nesle, who would be familiar with the institution, made in favour of their merchants a covenant with the citizens of London in 1237, which provided, among other things, that they should be free to attend certain fairs held elsewhere; among these St Ives is specially mentioned and the Puy regulations also give as a reason for changing the date of the great feast that many members were obliged to attend the St Ives fair and so to be out of town.

[1] The Provençal references are given in a note by P. Meyer to his edition of the *Chanson de la Croisade contre les Albigeois*, II, 399.

Great importance was attached by the Puys to poetical form, and the poems crowned by them were for the most part variations upon a theme already worn threadbare by the troubadours. Probably the productions of the London Puy, if any had survived, would be found similar in character to those of the continental fraternities. It has, however, its importance in the history of the English lyric, as one of the channels by which a knowledge of continental stanza form was brought to this country. If merchants from northern France could thus continue their interest in poetry, it is reasonable to think that southern Frenchmen would act in the same way.

Conversely, English wool and woollen fabrics were famous on the Continent; Peire Cardinal[1] says of the Jacobins that they abandon the hair shirt which is too rough for them and wear soft tunics woven of English wool:

> Per mols gonels testutz de lan' engleza
> Laisson celitz, car trop aspres lur es.

The opening lines of this poem refer to the delicacy of English work:

> Ab motz suptils, plans plus c'obra d'Engles.

English money was current in southern France: Bertran de Born[2] couples *esterlis e tornes*, English and French money. English soldiers appeared on

[1] Bartsch, *Gr.* 335, 1.

[2] Ed. Stimming, p. 199, note to II, 16. Sterling was the name of a coin; for the derivation from Easterling and the connection with the Hanseatic merchants, see *New English Dict.*

the Continent with sufficient frequency to earn an opprobrious epithet, which the troubadour Peire d'Auvergne[1] uses, *Engles coutz*, Englishmen with tails. The beauty of Englishwomen is mentioned in a stanza quoted by Nostradamus[2] and attributed to the Emperor Frederic II:

Plas my cavallier Francés,
  E la donna Catallana,
E l'onrar del Gynoés
  E la cour de Kastellana,
Lou cantar Provensallés,
  E la dansa Trivyzana,
E lou corps Aragonnés,
  E la perla Julliana,
Las mans e kara d'Angles
  E lou donzel de Thuscana.

Amanieu de Sescas, in his *Ensenhamen de la Donzela*, gives a young lady advice upon the art of making conversation at table and selects the same subject:

E si fort vos enueia
son solatz e · us fa nueia,
demandatz li novelas;
"Cals donas son pus belas,
o Gascas o Englezas?"
E s'il vos ditz; "Guasconas,"
respondetz ses temor;
"Senher, sal vostr' onor,

[1] Ed. Zenker, Erlangen, 1900, p. 192. His note on the passage gives other references and discusses the origin of this expression, which was an insult current down to 1354.

[2] Jehan de Nostradamus, Chabaneau and Anglade's ed., Paris, 1913, p. 20 and notes, p. 301.

las donas d'Englaterra
son gensor d'autra terra."
E s'il vos ditz; "Englesa,"
respondetz; "Si no · us peza,
senher, genser es Guasca[1]."

"And if his company greatly wearies and bores you, ask of him some new thing (i.e. change the subject); 'Which ladies are the fairest, those of Gascony or of England?' And if he replies, 'Gascony ladies,' reply fearlessly, 'Sir, saving your honour, the ladies of England are fairer than those of any other land.' And if he says, 'English lady,' reply, 'Your pardon, sir, the Gascon lady is the fairer.'"

Thus, so far as intercourse went, there was no reason why Provençal influence should not have been exerted directly upon English literature. We have now to consider the interest which the troubadours themselves displayed in English affairs.

[1] Bartsch, *Chrest.* col. 356.

II

THE TROUBADOURS AND ENGLISH POLITICS

THERE is a possibility that Marcabrun, one of the earliest troubadours known to us, visited England in the reign of Henry I. William of Malmesbury says that Henry's wife, Matilda, was a great patroness of singers and gave them rich rewards. In the French *roman* Joufroi (13th century), the people of Poitou, when attacked by the Count of Toulouse, sent out messengers to find their lord and secure his help and one Marcabrun is said to have come to London,

Trovere fu molt de gran pris,

and to have had an interview with Henry I, who knew him well,

Bien le conuit le rois Henri
Qu'assez l'ot en sa cort veu[1].

There is no allusion in Marcabrun's remaining poems to confirm this statement: at any rate, the author of the *roman* saw no inherent improbability in the visit of a troubadour to London.

At the age of 21, Henry II possessed an empire only second in extent to that of the German Emperor. The lands added to his own hereditary possessions by his marriage with the divorced

[1] Quoted by Chabaneau, *Biographies des Troubadours*, p. 8.

Eleanor made him the lord of territory extending from the Loire to the Adour. Henry's court was the most brilliant in Europe, and London was then a centre of culture and letters, and the largest French-speaking city in Europe. Peter of Blois, who enjoyed Henry's favour, in a letter to the archbishop of Palermo, compares the learning of the King of Italy with that of the King of England, much to the advantage of the latter: "With the King of England there is school every day, constant conversation of the best scholars and discussion of questions." Eleanor's grandfather, William IX, was Count of Poitiers and Duke of Aquitaine; so far as can be seen from his own compositions and William of Malmesbury's account[1], he was a jovial sensualist, of adventurous and often unedifying life, who cared little for his reputation in the society of the time. He is the first troubadour known to us; his daughter-in-law, Beatrice the Countess of Die, was a famous *trobairitz* and Eleanor's court was the constant resort of troubadours, as it was in the time of her daughter, Marie of Champagne. This was the chief centre whence Provençal influence spread to the poets of northern France and among the troubadours who there appeared were Bernart de Ventadorn and Bertran de Born.

The former troubadour visited England in the train of Henry II: so much appears from his own words:

> Faihz es lo vers tot a randa,
> si que motz no · i descapdolha,

[1] See Pio Rajna's note in *Romania*, VI, 249.

outra la terra normanda,
part la fera mar prionda;
e si · m sui de midons lonhans,
vas se · m tira com azimans
la bela cui Deus defenda.

Si · l reis engles e · l ducs normans
o vol, eu la veirai abans
que l'iverns nos sobreprenda.

Pel rei sui engles e normans[1].

The allusions in this *chanso* show that it was written in the late autumn and the poet hopes to return to the Continent before winter sets in; but for the attraction of his love overseas, he would stay in England till Christmas. Henry's movements in the year 1155 are thought by Appel to suit these conditions best; the king spent the whole of that year in England and crossed to France early in 1156, reaching Rouen on February 2. It is possible that Chrétien de Troyes was at Henry's court together with Bernart. That he knew Bernart's poems is clear from imitations which appear in his own lyrics and in *Cliges*, line 4632, he alludes to the meeting between Henry and his barons at Wallingford on April 10, 1155. It is not un-

[1] Appel, no. 26. "My poem is composed quite to the end, so that not a word is missing, beyond the Norman land over the wild deep sea; and if I am far from my lady like a magnet the fair one draws me to her, whom may God protect. If the English king and Norman duke so wills it, I shall see her, before the winter surprises us. On the king's account I am an Englishman and a Norman."

For the discussion in full as to date, see the introduction to Appel, pp. lvi ff. The statement, p. lvi, "Bernart ist der einzige Trobador, von dem wir mit Sicherheit wissen, dass er in England war," requires modification.

reasonable to suppose that Bernart was brought to England by Eleanor for the coronation festivities which were celebrated in London with great splendour in the winter of 1154. So ardent a patroness of poetry and song would naturally bring troubadours in her train, and Bernart, her vassal, whose powers were known to her, was an obvious choice.

The reputation which Henry II enjoyed as a liberal patron of the troubadours appears in the didactic poem of Raimon Vidal of Bezaudun, *Abrils issi'e mays intrava*. In a retrospect of the happier times when troubadours were welcome, it is said

Et yeu auzi, com En Enricx,
Us reis d'Englaterra, donava
Cavals e muls e com sercava
Vas Lombardia · l pro marques
E de terras doas e tres,
On trobava baros assatz
Adreitz e ben acostumatz
E donadors vas totas mas.

"And I heard, how Sir Henry, a King of England, gave horses and mules as gifts and how he visited the brave marquis in Lombardy and two or three other countries, where he found many good barons, well mannered and liberal with both hands."

The marquis was Count Boniface I of Montferrat (1182–1204). The argument of the poem maintains that three qualities are necessary for perfection of character, nobility of feeling, common sense and knowledge,

E aquestz tres feiron N'Enric,
Un rei d'Englaterra, pujar.

. . . .

E sos filhs tres que noy oblit
N'Enric ni · N Richart ni · N Jaufre;
Car en lor ac dos tans de be
C'om non poiria d'un an dir.
Josta lui vic en cort venir
E domneys e guerras menar
E ac sazon sel que saup far
Noblezas ni valors ni sens.

"These three made Sir Henry, a King of England, to rise pre-eminent,...and his three sons whom I will not forget, Sir Henry, Sir Richard, and Sir Godfrey, for they possessed twice as many good qualities as a man could tell in a year. At his court I saw service of ladies and war prevail, and it was the right time for one who could do noble deeds and show capacity and understanding[1]."

In 1159 Henry began his campaign with Berengar IV of Barcelona and other nobles against Raimon of Toulouse (born 1134). Henry claimed the comté of Toulouse through his wife, Eleanor of Poitou, and when Raimon V refused to submit, he declared war and made alliance with Raimon Berengar of Barcelona at Blaye (Gironde) in 1159. The latter had a long-standing quarrel with Raimon and had already formed a league against him, on August 20, 1158, at Montpelier with Raimon Trencavel of Béziers and perhaps with Ermengarde of Narbonne and William of Montpelier. Henry arranged, to cement the alliance, that his son Richard (later Cœur de Lion) should hold the duchy of Guyenne and marry Berengaria, daughter of the Count of Barcelona. Henry then returned to England; he crossed with his nobles to the

[1] Ed. W. Bohs, Erlangen, 1903, ll. 189 ff., 273 ff. See also ll. 859 ff.

Continent about mid-Lent to begin hostilities. Louis VII of France attempted to intervene through his sister Constance who was sister-in-law of Raimon V, but without result, though he had a personal interview with Henry at Tours. Henry concentrated his forces at Poitiers towards the end of June; a second and third meeting with Louis proved barren of result. Louis then went to Toulouse in person and put the town in a state of defence, while Henry marched south, devastating the country and capturing a number of castles belonging to the Count of Toulouse, including Verdun and Castelnau. Meanwhile Raimon Berengar was in Spain, but at the beginning of August his forces joined Henry, who then besieged Toulouse, but out of respect for Louis did not attempt to storm the town. At the end of September he withdrew, leaving garrisons in the castles he had taken.

Peire d'Auvergne refers to these events with obvious sympathy for the Count of Toulouse, perhaps because he had not found the other side as generous as he expected.

> Qu'ab un jovencel valen
> avetz lai guerr'e conten,
> tal que fier si de sa lansa
> que d'aquelhs Engles coüitz
> ni dels vostres esternutz
> non a paor ni doptansa[1].

"For with a valiant youth you there have war and strife, such a one who strikes so hard with his lance that he has no fear or dread of those English with tails nor of your sneezing."

[1] Zenker, *Peire von Auvergne*, p. 110.

Bertran de Born of Périgord, who was born between 1135 and 1140, has been called the evil genius of Henry II's reign. Such a term greatly exaggerates his historical importance. He showed much adroitness in stirring up strife; *fetz mesclar lo paire e·l filh d'Englaterra* is one of the few historically accurate statements in his Provençal biography and the king no doubt regarded him as a dangerous man. But the legends which gathered round his personality and the genius of Dante have given him a greater place in history than he deserves. His intimacy with Henry's sons is shown by the fact that he has a *senhal* or pseudonym for each of them. Richard is *Oc e No* (Yea and Nay), Geoffrey is *Rassa* and Henry is perhaps denoted by *Marinier*. The last named was crowned as heir to the throne in Westminster on June 15, 1170, and was afterwards known as the "young king." He then received the government of Anjou and Maine and Richard that of Aquitaine and Poitou. We do not know how the intimacy between Bertran and the princes began, but as they often made a long stay in his neighbourhood it is not surprising that they should have known one another; the fact that the troubadour took their side against the king is evidence that the friendship between them was close and there was time for it to develop after 1163 when Eleanor ruled in Bordeaux as regent for her three sons; nor can we leave out of account a certain personal charm which Bertran undoubtedly possessed, apart from his fondness for the knightly pursuits of his time and his reputation as a troubadour.

Richard was not a popular duke; his severity in dealing with refractory barons produced sporadic revolts among his vassals. One of these occurred in 1182 and Bertran then supported a coalition against Richard with voice and influence, though he took no personal part in the struggle. It was probably upon this matter that he quarrelled with his brother Constantine, who shared with him possession of the castle of Autafort. Constantine was a lover of peace and declined to be led into a struggle with his overlord Richard. Bertran succeeded in turning him out of the castle and seizing the whole estate for himself, and though Constantine made various applications to Henry and the princes to secure his reinstatement, Bertran remained in possession.

Richard refused to do homage to his brother Henry after the coronation of 1170, on the ground that as duke of Aquitaine he was a vassal of the French king. The brothers had quarrelled about the possession of the castle of Clairvaux and the Aquitanian barons, who hated Richard, had offered to secure the dukedom for Henry, if he would support a rebellion for that purpose. By the end of 1182 this tension had reached breaking point. The young king accepted the proposal of the Aquitanian barons and formed a league with Geoffrey to drive Richard out of his possessions. Bertran joined Henry's party; he seems to have had a real liking for the generous and pliable young king and a strong dislike of the gusty temper and violent methods of Richard. In one poem he enumerates the members of the league, challenges Richard to combat and reminds Henry of the quarrel concerning the castle of Clairvaux. War began; Henry invaded Poitou and Aquitaine and Richard could not make head against his superior numbers. But the king intervened with an army from England and forced the brothers to make peace: he settled the dispute concerning the castle of Clairvaux by taking possession of it himself. So sudden a termination of a promising uproar was far from satisfactory to Bertran, and he expressed his disgust in no measured terms:

D'un sirventes no · m chal far lonhor ganda,
Tal talan ai que · l diga e que l'espanda,
Quar n'ai razo tan novela e tan granda
De · l jove rei qu'a fenit sa demanda
So frair Richart, puois sos pairs lo comanda;
    Tan es forsatz!
Puois n'Aenrics terra no te ni manda,
    Sia reis de · ls malvatz[1]!

"I can no longer delay composing a sirventes, so great is my desire to say it and spread it abroad; I have indeed so new and strong a theme in the young king who has withdrawn the claim he made upon his brother Richard, because his father so orders; so wanting is he in independence! As Sir Henry neither holds nor rules land, let him be king of the dastards!"

The peace was of no long duration. The revolted barons would not recognise a convention concluded without consideration of their interests. The league was revived, but upon this occasion Henry and Geoffrey turned against their father. Bertran again

[1] Stimming, *Bertran von Born*, Halle a. S. 1892, no. 6.

joined them and the *sirventes* which he produced was composed at the desire of the young king: he admits that their cause was unjust.

De mo senhor lo rei annat
Conosc que an siei filh pechat,
  Que de · l sojorn d'Englaterra
L'an aoras dos ans lonhat;
De totz lo tenc per enjanat
Mas quan de Johan ses Terra[1].

"I recognise that as regards my lord the elder king his sons have sinned, for they have kept him now two years from a stay in England; I regard him as deceived by them all, except by John Lackland."

The young king caught enteric fever and died in the castle of Martel on June 11, 1183, aged 29. His death was deeply felt by Bertran who was attached to him by affection as well as by self-interest. The *planh* in which he laments his death is a fine composition, but is surpassed by one usually attributed to Bertran, but more probably written by Peire Vidal.

Si tuit li dol e · lh plor e · lh marrimen
E las dolors e · lh dan e · lh chaitivier
Que om anc auzis en est segle dolen
Fossen ensems, semblaran tot leugier
Contra la mort de · l jove rei engles,
Don rema pretz e jovens doloros
E · l mons oscurs e teintz e tenebros
Sems de tot joi, ples de tristor e d'ira[2].

[1] Stimming, no. 7. I adopt the reading of Thomas in the 5th line of the stanza, instead of Stimming's "de · l tot lo · n tenh." "Two years" is an exaggeration: Henry had left England on March 3, 1182.

[2] Stimming, no. 9. Translation, Barbara Smythe, *Trobador Poets*, London, 1911, p. 79; Stronski, *Folquet de Marseille*, p. xii.

"If all the grief and tears and misery
And all the sad world's wretchedness and woe
And sorrow were united, there would be
No fitting lamentation even so
Made for the death of the young English king,
Whereat the young and noble are dismayed,
And all the world is plunged in gloom and shade
Deprived of joy and filled with grief and sorrow."

The revolted barons were now without a leader, the league collapsed and the members made the best terms they could gain from the wrathful Richard. Bertran did not escape; Richard devastated his estates, captured his castle of Autafort with the help of King Alfonso of Aragon and restored it to Bertran's brother Constantine. The well-known scene related in the Provençal *razo* which represents Bertran in the King of England's tent after the capture of his castle, securing his pardon by a reference to the young king's death, has no foundation in fact. Henry II was not present at the capture of Autafort and Bertran was for some time deprived of his possessions. He was eventually reinstated, but of the circumstances no reliable account remains. By some means he succeeded in securing a reconciliation with Richard and remained faithful to his interests for the future. Shortly after the death of the young king, Henry II proposed that Richard should hand over the lordship of Aquitaine to John. Richard declined and the king authorised John to invade his territory. Geoffrey joined forces with John and so the brothers were again at war. Bertran's *sirventes* on this occasion urged Richard to resistance and advised him even to claim the English throne; he bitterly reproached Geoffrey for deserting his Aquitanian allies in the previous struggle, and regarded his present enterprise as hopeless.

To this time also belongs a poem in which Bertran reproaches Geoffrey for failing to keep an appointment with some lady and refers to his designs on Richard's land:

S·il coms Jaufres no s'eslonha,
Peitau aura e Guasconha,
Si tot no sap domneiar[1].

"If Count Geoffrey does not run away, he will have Poitou and Gascony, although he does not know how to behave to ladies."

The war went on during 1184 until Henry summoned the three brothers to London and patched up a peace, under which Richard was to keep Aquitaine. He, however, invaded Brittany in the following year, and Geoffrey made overtures to the French king for help in his designs upon Anjou. These excursions and alarms were ended for the moment by Geoffrey's death on August 19, 1186. Seven months after his death, on March 29, 1187, the Countess Constance, his wife, gave birth to a son, who was christened Arthur, to please the Bretons with a reference to their early legends. Peire Vidal refers to this event:

E cel que long' atendensa
Blasma, fai gran falhizo;
Qu'er an Artus li Breto,
On avian lor plevensa[2].

[1] Stimming, no. 39.
[2] Anglade, *Les poésies de Peire Vidal*, Paris, 1913, no. xxviii, l. 46.

"He who blames long waiting makes a great mistake; for now the Bretons have their Arthur where they had set their hope."

And again:

> Que pos Artus an cobrat en Bretanha,
> Non es razos que mais jois mi sofranha[1].

"For since the Bretons have recovered Arthur, there is no reason why joy should fail me henceforward."

To events of this year another stanza in the same *chanso* appears to allude: it also stigmatises the stinginess of Philippe Auguste, who was not a favourite with troubadours.

> De lai on creisso · l fau
> Mi ven us jauzimens,
> Don sui gais e jauzens,
> Qu'onra · l nom de Peitau,
> E ja · l fals recrezens,
> Cobes mal despendens,
> No pot re conquistar
> Per soven penchenar.

"From there where the beeches grow, joyous news comes to me and cheers me: for he honours the name of Poitou (Richard took the Cross in 1187 as Count of Poitiers), and henceforward the cowardly hypocrite, the miser who cannot spend, can conquer nothing, however often he combs his hair."

But in 1187 war between England and France seemed inevitable. Apart from Geoffrey's intrigues, there was a dispute concerning the dowry which Margaret had brought to the young Henry on her marriage and the question of her jointure, which

[1] Anglade, no. xxiii, l. 29.

Henry declined to pay. Attacks by the French on Normandy and by English forces under Richard on Toulouse and disputes concerning the wardship of Brittany were additional sources of bitterness. On February 17, 1187, Henry crossed to France with an army and after a futile conference at Nonancourt war began and ended in the truce of Châteauroux on June 23. This was brought about by the papal legates who were urging Christendom to cease private quarrels and unite for the delivery of the Holy Land, the news from which had spread consternation through Europe.

Bertran was involved in these events and his interests are expressed in two *sirventes*, in both of which his anxiety for war and his disgust at the conclusion of the armistice are expressed with characteristic vigour; he especially states that the French king was induced to agree to the armistice because his Champagne contingents refused to advance to the attack, for the reason that they had been bribed by Henry. The news of Saladin's capture of Jerusalem (September 29, 1187) roused desire for a crusade in all quarters. Richard was one of the first to take the cross and Bertran praised his example in a crusade poem, of which only one half remains to us. But Richard's vacillating mind was incapable of keeping one object steadily in view. After Henry had returned to England on February 26, 1188, to raise money for the crusade, Richard was informed that Godfrey of Lusignan had treacherously killed one of his Poitevin friends. When he started to avenge this deed, some of his own barons again revolted and no sooner had he suppressed this rising and driven Godfrey out of his province, than he was involved in a quarrel with the Count of Toulouse who had ill-treated some merchants of Aquitaine. Richard's diplomacy never went beyond the use of fire and sword; he invaded the count's territory with such energy and ruthlessness that Philippe Auguste soon received most urgent requests for help from his hard-pressed vassal. Bertran took no part in these campaigns, but he expressed his satisfaction in two *sirventes*:

E sai Richartz pren lebres e leos,
Que no · n rema per plas ni per boissos,
Enanz los fai dos e dos remaner
Per sa forza, qu'us no · s n'ausa mover,
E cuja be penre d'aissi enan
Las grans aiglas ab los esmerilhos
Et ab buzacs metr' austors en soan.

E · l reis Felips chassa lai ab falcos
Sos perdigals e · ls petitz auzelos,
E siei home no l'ausan dire · l ver
Quar pauc e pauc si laissa dechazer
Sai a · n Richart, que l'a tolgut ogan
Engolesme, don s'es fachs poderos,
E Tolosa, qu'el te sobre deman.

E puois non es per sa terra iros,
Membre · lh sa sor e · l maritz orgolhos,
Que la laissa e no la vol tener;
Aquest forfachs mi sembla desplazer,
E tot ades que s'en vai perjuran,
Que · l reis navars l'a sai dat per espos
A sa filha, per que l'ant'es plus gran[1].

"And here Richard catches hares and lions, so that none

[1] Stimming, no. 20.

remain in plain or wood, but he makes them remain in pairs by his power, so that none dares to move, and he thinks henceforward of catching great eagles with hawks and of putting falcons to shame with bustards. And there King Philip hunts partridges and little birds with falcons, and his men dare not tell him the truth, for by degrees he is here letting himself be overthrown by Sir Richard, for this year he has taken from him Angoulême, of which he has made himself master and Toulouse, which he claims. And since he is not angry on account of his land, let him remember his sister and the proud husband who leaves her and will not keep her. That insult methinks displeases and above all that the fact that he continues to perjure himself, for the King of Navarre has given him as husband to his daughter, wherefore the shame is greater."

Bertran thus attempted to inflame passion by reminding Philippe Auguste of the fact that Richard who had been betrothed to his sister Alais in 1174 had abandoned her for Berengaria of Navarre. Philippe began war with Richard in the middle of June 1188.

Other troubadours were also roused to proclaim the crusade by the news that a century's work had been undone: Aimeric de Belenoi thus refers to Richard:

> Selh cui dieus det sen e vigor
> et a de totz bos pretz l'onor,
> qu'es coms et er reys apellatz,
> ajuda premiers e secor
> al sepulcre on dieus fo pauzatz;
> E dieus per sa gran pitansa,
> si cum es vera Trinitatz,
> lo guit e · l fass' amparanza
> sobrels fals Turcx desbateiatz[1].

[1] K. Lewent, *Das altprovenzalische Kreuzlied*, Erlangen, 1905,

"He to whom God gave understanding and strength, and who is honoured with all noble qualities, who is count and will be called king, he is the first to help and succour the sepulchre in which God was laid. And may God in His great mercy, as He is the true Trinity, guide him and give him protection against the false unbaptised Turks."

So also Giraut de Bornelh in a vigorous appeal, invoking shame upon all who stay at home, speaks with confidence of Richard:

E · l coms Richartz es be garnitz;
C'als seus aïtz,
qui que · l n'envei,
S'es tals afars mesclatz
Que ben es grans, e sia · n Deus lauzatz[1]!

"And the Count Richard is well equipped; for against his enemies, however he may be envied for it, such a business has been set on foot that it is a great matter and God be praised for it."

Henry II died on July 6, 1189 and Richard succeeded him. He spent the first year of his reign in securing his position, and Bertran reminded him and Philip of their crusade vows by holding up the example of Conrad, Marquis of Montferrat, who had aroused general admiration by his brave and successful resistance to the victorious Saladin.

Senher Conratz, ieu sai dos reis qu'estan
D'ajudar vos, ara entendatz qui:
Lo reis Felips es l'us, quar vai doptan
Lo rei Richart, e cel lui dopt' aissi;
Ar fos usquecs d'els en boia

pp. 19 and 101. Stronski doubts the attribution to A. de Belenoi; his edition of *Folquet de Marseille*, p. 19 of introduction. See also *Ann. du Midi*, XVIII, year 1906, p. 478.

[1] Kolsen, *Giraut de Bornelh*, Halle a. S. 1910, p. 390.

D'en Saladi, puois van dieu galian,
Quar son crozat e d'anar mot no fan[1].

"Lord Conrad, I know two kings who are slow to help you; now hear who they are; King Philip is one, for he doubts King Richard and the latter doubts him likewise: now would they were both in the chains of Sir Saladin, for they keep deceiving God, since they have taken the cross and speak no word of going."

Other troubadours felt similar doubts, in view of the notorious instability of Richard's character. Gaucelm Faidit tells him that he cannot have the credit of a crusader by staying at home:

Al comte mon senhor vuelh dire
Qu'aissi cum ac primiers l'onor,
Gard que Dieus li sia grazire
Qu'al passar cont om la lauzor[2].

"To my lord the count I would say that even as he has been the first to have the honour (of taking the cross), let him see to it that God is grateful to him, for the glory is only counted from the moment of departure."

Elsewhere he complains that his lady and the English king keep him from Syria, the one by love and the other by the fact that he does not help the troubadour's lack of means. Peirol alludes to the defence of Conrad of Montferrat and complains that quarrels between Richard and Philip delay the crusade[3].

Pons de Capduelh, a troubadour of wealth and standing, no doubt expressed a general desire when he said:

[1] Stimming, no. 21.
[2] Bartsch, *Grundriss*, 167, 58. Mahn, *Gedichte*, 499, 500.
[3] Mahn, *Werke*, II, 5.

Ben volgra que · l reis dels Frances
E · l rei engles fezesson patz,
Et aquel fora plus honratz
Per dieu, que primiers la volgues[1].

"I earnestly wish that the king of the French and the English king would make peace, and he would be the more honoured by God who should be the first to desire it."

As a matter of fact, Richard's mind was entirely bent on the crusade adventure: he went to England for his coronation because, unlike his father, he loved pomp and show and also to raise money for the expedition. But he was rather a Frenchman than an Englishman; he had previously paid only two short visits to England in 1176 and 1184. Before starting he had a meeting with Philippe Auguste and a further conference upon his return, when the outstanding differences between them were patched up. Bertran refers to the cession of Gisors which Louis VII had ceded with the Norman Vexin, the territory between the Epte and the Andelle, as the portion of the young Queen Margaret and which Henry II obstinately refused to surrender.

Si · l reis Felips, reis de · ls Frances,
A volgut a Richart donar
Gisortz, aut luoc et aut paes,
Richartz l'en deu fort merceiar;
Mas si Felips de · l mieu cor fos,
Richartz no mouria · ls talos
A son dan senes encontrar;
E puois no · l vol, lais s'en ferrar.

[1] Ed. Napolski, Halle, 1879, no. xxvi (crusade poem). K. Lewent, *Das altprovenzalische Kreuzlied*, p. 30.

Papiols, sias tan cochos,
Di · m en Richart qu'el es leos,
E · l reis Felips anhels mi par,
Qu'aissi · s laissa deseretar[1].

"If King Philip, king of the French, has been willing to give Gisors to Richard, a high place and country, Richard should be very grateful to him; but if Philip were of my mind, Richard would not stir to hurt him without meeting him; and as he will not, he lets himself be chained. Papiol, hasten quickly and tell Richard from me that he is a lion and King Philip seems to me a lamb as he thus allows himself to be disinherited."

Richard's departure in 1190 dispelled the doubts in circulation concerning the reality of his intentions. Folquet of Marseilles thus triumphantly praises him:

E qui · l bon rei Richart qui vol qu'ieu chan
blasmet per so quar non passet dese,
ar l'en desmen si que chascus o ve;
qu'areire · s trais per miels salhir enan:
qu'el era coms, ar es rix reis ses fi,
quar bon socors fai Dieus a bon voler;
e s'ie · n dis ben al crozar, ieu dis ver,
et ar veim o, per qu'adonc no menti[2].

"And if anyone blamed the good King Richard, who wishes me to sing, because he did not at once make the passage (to the Holy Land), now I give him the lie, as each one sees; for he withdrew, the better to leap forward; he was indeed a count, now he is a wealthy absolute king, for God gives good support to good-will, and as I spoke well of him at his taking of the cross, I spoke the truth, and now we see it, because then I did not lie."

The previous poem of which Folquet speaks has

[1] Stimming, no. 23.
[2] Stronski, no. x, and introd. pp. 21–23.

not been preserved. This composition may have been sung to Richard himself as he passed through Marseilles on July 31, 1190. He left the town on August 7. Philip had agreed to take the indemnity of 20,000 marks which Henry II had offered, plus 4000 for his "expenses." This question was reopened by the appearance of Berengaria when both kings were at Messina; it was then arranged that Richard and his heirs should keep Gisors. Probably Bertran's poem refers to this last occasion. Philip then realised that Richard would not marry Alais and his conduct may well be characterised as lamblike. The poet had not been able to join in the crusade for lack of means and he draws a dismal picture of France without her nobles and lords. Moreover, before the kings had actually started, Bertran had been careful, so far as we know, to avoid making mischief between them, in order not to prejudice the prospects of the crusade. Lastly, the terms Lamb and Lion are said by Richard of Devizes to have been given to the two kings by the inhabitants of Messina; the excited mob, who jeered at Richard and asked him questions about his tail, had every reason after the sack of Messina to remember the old legend that the lion lashed his flanks with his tail before attacking, as a sharp point in the end of it thus spurred him to anger[1].

Richard's prowess as a crusader became prover-

[1] Richard of Devizes 397. "Graeculi enim et Siculi omnes.... Anglos caudatos nominabant." See p. 32. For this and other uses to which the lion puts his tail see Philippe de Thaün, *Bestiaire*, ll. 93 ff.

bial. When Lanfranc Cigala appealed to Henry III to take the cross and come to the help of the Holy Land, he reminded him of Richard: "e del valen Rei Richart li sovegna[1]." Much grief was aroused in the troubadour world by Richard's imprisonment, of which Peire Vidal speaks. This troubadour is said to have joined the crusaders in Sicily; to judge from the gentle hint in the *tornada* of a *chanso* written before the crusader started, he seems to have been as impecunious as Bertran de Born, and also doubtful of the reality of Richard's intention.

> Lai vir mon chant, al rei celestial,
> Cui devem tug onrar et obezir,
> Et es be dreitz que l'anem lai servir
> On conquerrem la vid' esperital;
> Que · l sarrazi desleial, canineu,
> L'an tout son regn'e destruita sa pleu,
> Que sazit an la crotz e · l monumen:
> Don devem tug aver gran espaven.
>
> Coms de Peiteus, de vos mi clam a Deu
> E Deus a me per aquel eis coven,
> El de sa crotz et eu de mon argen.
>
> Coms de Peiteus, bels senher, vos et eu
> Avem lo pretz de tota l'autra gen,
> Vos de ben far et eu de dir lo gen.

"I address my song to the King of Heaven whom we should all honour and obey; it is right that we should go and serve there where we shall gain spiritual life; for the treacherous and cruel Saracens have taken from Him His realm and destroyed His empire; they have seized the cross and the sepulchre and that should make us all tremble.

[1] Bertoni, *Trovatori d'Italia*, p. 351.

Count of Poitou, I complain of you to God and God likewise complains to me, He of His cross and I of my money. Count of Poitou, you and I are praised by the rest of men, you for good deeds and I for good words."

Peire Vidal thus refers to Richard's imprisonment:

> Et anc pos lo guitz de Deu frais
> Non auzim pois l'Emperador
> Creisser de pretz ni de barnat.
> Mas pero s'oimais laiss' en fat
> Richart, pos en sa preizon es,
> Lor esquern en faran Engles.

"Since the emperor has thrown off the yoke of God, we have not heard that his reputation and honour have increased. If however he foolishly abandons Richard, as he is in his prison, the English will hold him up to scorn."

> Mas al derrier sospir
> Ja no · l valra feunia
> Plus que fetz don Enric,
> Quan camjava nessic
> E · l bon Richart aunic
> E Deu que n'envazic.

"But at the last gasp his wickedness will help him no more than it helped Lord Henry (the emperor) when he foolishly changed and put shame upon the good Richard and attacked God[1]."

Of Richard's song in his captivity, both a French and a Provençal version are extant[2]. The story

[1] Anglade, no. xxiv, 49; xxxii, 27; xxxviii, 31. Also the *Monk of Montaudon*, ed. Philippson, Halle, 1873, no. xii.

[2] Richard's poem has been repeatedly printed: Leroux, *Chants historiques*, I, 56–59; Tarbé, *Œuvres de Blondel de Nesle*, Rheims, 1862, p. 117; Bartsch, *Chrest. ancien français*, p. 185; Raynouard, *Choix*, IV, 183; Mahn, *Werke der Troub.* I, 129; Bartsch, *Prov. Lesebuch* (1st ed.), p. 78. Probably the French version is the older. The song is in the form of a *retroencha* (French *rotrouenge*) which

of Blondel de Nesle's discovery of Richard's prison is pure fiction[1]. Blondel probably belonged to Nesle in Picardy, not far from Peronne; his poems contain no allusions which enable us to assign any one of them to any particular year and are entirely love poems, providing good examples of the results of Provençal influence upon northern French poetry. Unhistorical as the Blondel legend is, the fact that it gained credence at an early date may be regarded as evidence, if any were required, that such a part was not impossible for a troubadour to play. Popular fiction is indicative of the ideas current at

seems not to have differed greatly from the usual *chanso* except for a refrain. Very few examples are extant in Provençal and the form seems for some unknown reason to have been regarded as best handled in French. Possibly for this reason, as Crescini notes, Gaucelm Faidit wrote his refrain *chanso* in French and the Anglo-Norman example is probably not a translation. If this view of the *retroencha* existed, Richard would have naturally chosen French. (See Appendix, p. 152.)

For Richard's *sirventes* against the Dauphin of Auvergne, which is also in French, see below. Chabaneau, *Biogr. des Troub.* p. 55, says: "un ms. aujourd'hui perdu, qui a appartenu à Fr. Redi, renfermait au moins une pièce, toute provençale, du roi Richard. Un Chroniqueur anglais, Geoffroi Winisauf, parle d'une chanson que Richard composa, dans la Terre-Sainte, pour répondre à celle que Henri, duc de Bourgogne, avait fait contre lui. Cette chanson ne nous est pas parvenue. Il est plus que probable qu'elle était en français. Voici le passage de Winisauf, d'après Tarbé, qui le cite p. 113 de son édition de Blondel de Nesle.

"Postquam haec invidiosa adinventio passim per exercitum frequentaretur, rex (Ricardus) nimium super eo commotus, consimili tantum arbitratus est infligendam vindictam talione. Cantavit igitur et ipse nonnulla de ipsis, sed non plurimum laboravit in adinventionem, quia superabundans suppetebat materia." *Gaufr. Ricardi itin.* lib. vi, c. 8. Also in Diez, *Leben u. Werke*, p. 88.

[1] A full discussion of the subject is given in Dr Leo Wiese's edition of *Blondel de Nesle*, Dresden, 1904.

the time of its formation; if it were not in focus with the mental prepossessions of its auditors, it would not be circulated and the story illustrates the importance of troubadours and their poetry in the social life of the age.

Richard's return was greeted with delight by the troubadours to whom he was a valuable patron. Bertran de Born proclaimed his hope that the barons who had created disturbances during the king's absence would receive their deserts; he upbraided the emperor Henry VI for imprisoning a crusader on his homeward journey, an act of which his father, Frederick Barbarossa, would never have been guilty, and which was punishable with excommunication.

Papiols, ja · n Frederis
No feira aital barganha
Com fetz sos filhs n'Aenris
Quan pres romieus ab bordos[1].

"Papiol, never would Sir Frederick have done such an act as his son Sir Henry did, when he captured a pilgrim with his staff."

In a second *sirventes* of the same kind, the troubadour expects the king's arrival and the resumption of war: he hopes that Richard will show no mercy to the rebellious; he is no mercenary bard; let no one think that he composes poems to sell; a man should support his lord's cause.

E no · us cujetz qu'ieu fassa motz a vendre,
Mas per ric bar deu hom tot jorn contendre[2].

At some date between April and July 1195, Folquet of Marseilles wrote a crusade poem in

[1] Stimming, no. 24. [2] *Ibid.* no. 25.

support of the Pope's effort to revive the crusade in Palestine.

> Doncx, nostre baro que fan
> ni · l reys engles cui Dieus sal?
> Cuid' aver fait son jornal?
> Mout i aura lag engan
> s'el a fag la messio
> et autre fan la preiso!
> Que l'emperaire · s percassa
> cum Dieus cobres sa reio;
> que primiers cre que · i secor
> si Dieus li rent sa honor:
> be · s taing, tan es rix lo dos,
> qu'aitals sia · l guizerdos[1].

"What, then, are our barons doing and the English king, whom may God preserve? Does he think that he has accomplished his task? There will be a very ugly piece of deceit, if he has borne the expense and another takes the prize. For the emperor is making efforts that God may recover His country; he will be the first to bring help to it, if God grants him his land (as a fief); it is fitting, as the gift is so rich, that the reward should be likewise."

After a violent quarrel with the Papacy, the emperor Henry VI had suddenly and entirely changed his attitude; on March 31, 1195, he had secretly taken the cross and on Easter Day, two days later, he had proclaimed the crusade at Bari; he had also sent ambassadors to the Pope, to inform him of these pious intentions. Folquet appears to be aware of the fact that Richard had solemnly promised to renew the crusade, both when he left Palestine, in October 1192 and after his liberation

[1] Stronski, *Folquet de Marseille*, Cracovie, 1910, no. xviii. See also pp. 173–182 for a general discussion of previous interpretations.

from captivity in February 1194, of which promise the Church had not failed to remind him. Folquet considers that Richard will suffer a great injustice, if he allows the emperor to conquer the Holy Land, in view of the vast sums which Richard had expended both in preparation and for his ransom. The troubadour regards the emperor's crusade as an act of expiation, part of which was the use for religious purposes of the ransom extorted from Richard. He does not share Richard's opinion, that his past expenditure was sufficiently great to absolve him from the obligation of any further crusading efforts. God, as elsewhere in the troubadours, is regarded as the feudal lord of the Holy Land, and the emperor will hold a predominant position in the East, if he is invested with this fief. The *chanso* concludes with reproaches to Philippe Auguste for his desertion of the crusade in 1192.

Richard's other remaining poem, a *sirventes* to the Dauphin of Auvergne, was evoked by the events of 1195–6[1]. The emperor's intrigues had again set Richard and Philip at variance and a sharp struggle began which was ended by the treaty signed at Vaudreuil on January 15th under which Richard surrendered Auvergne, receiving Quercy in exchange. The Dauphin of Auvergne and his cousin Guy, the Count of Auvergne, thus became Philip's vassals and were far from pleased with the change. Their forebodings were confirmed when Philip bought a fortress in Auvergne and seized the town of Issoire. They applied to Richard who persuaded

[1] See *Ann. du Midi*, XVIII, 1906, p. 479.

them to revolt, but when they acted in reliance upon his promises, Richard pleaded a new convention with the French king and refused to help them. The cousins were forced to make the best terms they could with Philip. When Richard was again at war with Philip, he did not scruple to ask the cousins for help. They naturally declined and Richard sent a *sirventes* to the Dauphin, unreasonably taunting and upbraiding him for his refusal. The Dauphin replied in similar terms and with more effective arguments.

He concluded a convention with Philip in 1199, under the terms of which he recovered the places which the French king had seized. The point of literary interest in the controversy is the fact that a challenge in French provokes an answer in Provençal.

It was in the course of this war between Richard and Philip, that the English king expected some help from Alfonso VIII of Castile, who had married his sister Eleanor. Bertran de Born obviously expected the arrival of the Spaniards.

> Miei sirventes vuolh far de · ls reis amdos,
> Qu'en brieu veirem qu'aura mais chavaliers,
> De · l valen rei de Castela, n'Anfos,
> Qu'auch dir que ve e volra soudadiers;
> Richartz metra a muois et a sestiers
> Aur et argen e te s'a benananza
> Metr' e donar e no vol sa fianza,
> Anz vol guerra mais que qualha esparviers.

"I wish to make a half sirventes of the two kings: in a short time we shall see which of the two has more knights; for I hear of the bold King of Castile, the lord Alfonso, that he is coming and will want soldiers. Richard will pour out gold and silver by the bushel and he considers spending and giving a piece of good fortune and does not desire his security; on the contrary, he is more desirous of war than is the sparrow-hawk of the quail[1]."

Alfonso had been heavily defeated by the Moors at Alarcos on July 19, 1195, and was unable to keep any promise he may have made to Richard. The troubadour Gavaudan invited Richard to join a crusade to Spain to help the Christians against the Moors[2].

> Emperaire, vos o aujatz,
> El reys de Fransa, e sos cozis,
> El reys engles, coms peitavis,
> Qu'al rey d'Espanha socorratz.

"Hear them, oh Emperor! (Henry VI) and you, King of France and you, his cousin, King of England, Count of Poitou, come to the help of the King of Spain."

The "cousin" (in a wide sense of the term which is not unusual) was unable to accede to this appeal.

In 1196 Richard was at variance with his nephew Arthur concerning the latter's position in Brittany: Richard wished to act as Arthur's guardian, and Henry II after Geoffrey's death had obliged Constance, the Countess of Brittany, to marry Ralph III, Earl of Chester, with a view to maintaining the connection between Normandy and Brittany, the earl holding a hereditary title in Normandy. The countess soon separated from her second husband and ruled Brittany in practical independence. When Richard

[1] Stimming, no. 26. [2] Jeanroy, *Romania*, vol. XXXIV, no. 9.

demanded the wardship of his nephew, the countess set out to meet him, but was captured on the way by her husband. The Bretons took up arms to liberate their countess and Richard invaded the country to secure the person of Arthur, whom the Bretons sent to Paris for safety[1]. The *sirventes* referring to these events may not have been composed by Bertran de Born, who had entered the monastery of Dalon before January 8, 1196, when his name is mentioned as a witness in the cartulary. One of his sons who bore his name was possibly the author of it.

Breto son fors de guaranda
E son d'onor bas,
Quar us coms de Saint Tomas
Entret en Bresilianda:
Be paron de bo cor blos
E tornat de sus en jos,
Quar lor Artus demandan frevolmen:
No·n dirai plus, quar negus no m'enten.

"The Bretons are without guarantee and are void of honour, for a count of St Thomas (i.e. an English nobleman, the Earl of Chester) enters Bresilianda (a wood in Brittany, often mentioned in Arthurian romances and so a name for the province in general); they appear lacking in courage and wholly bewildered, for they foolishly demand their Arthur (the mythical king, who was to return and liberate them): I will say no more, for no one understands me."

Richard's death was a cause of great regret to all troubadours, to whom he had been a lavish

[1] So Ramsay, *Angevin Empire*, p. 350. Stimming gives the date 1197 and states that Arthur was hidden in the hills of the peninsula and that the Bretons appealed to Philip for help. (p. 42 of his ed.)

patron: his liberality is often contrasted with the meanness of Philippe Auguste[1]. The *planh* composed by Gaucelm Faidit is indicative of general feeling.

> Fortz chausa es que tot lo maior dan
> e·l maior dol, las! qu'ieu anc mais agues,
> e so don dei tostemps planher ploran,
> m'aven a dir en chantan e retraire,
> car selh qu'era de valor caps e paire,
> lo rics valens Richartz, reys dels Engles,
> es mortz; ai Dieus! quals perd'e quals dans es!
> Quant estrangz motz, quan salvatge a auzir!
> ben a dur cor totz hom qu'o pot suffrir.
>
> Mortz es lo reys, e son passat mil an
> qu'anc tan pros hom no fo, ni no·l vi res,
> ni mais non er nulhs hom del sieu semblan,
> tan larcs, tan pros, tan arditz, tals donaire;
> qu'Alichandres, lo reys qui venquet Daire,
> no cre que tan dones ni tan mezes
> ni anc Charles ni Artus tan valgues,
> qu'a tot lo mon se fes, qui·n vol ver dir,
> als us duptar et als autres grazir[2].

[1] It should be noted that the French king's motives were not necessarily those of parsimony. The Church taught that liberality to jongleurs was sin. So Rigord, *de Gestis Philippe Auguste* (*Recueil des historiens de France*, t. XVII, p. 21; Faral, p. 288): "cum in terra regum seu aliorum principum frequens turba histrionum convenire soleat, ut ab eis aurum, argentum, equos, seu vestes, quas saepe mutare consueverunt principes ab eis extorqueant, verba joculatoria variis adulationibus plena proferre nituntur...sed christianissimus rex Philippus Augustus, videns omnia ista esse vana et saluti animae contraria, instinctu Spiritus Sancti reducens ad memoriam quod a sanctis et religiosis viris quandoque didicerat, quod histrionibus dare daemonibus est immolare, mente promptissima Domino Deo promisit quod omnes vestes suas...pauperibus erogaret." See Part I, p. 2. An English version is quoted by Coulton, *Social Life in England*, p. 404.

[2] Appel, *Chrest. Prov.* no. 82.

Needs must I sing the chiefest woe and grief,
The hardest loss that ever I should bear,
For which I yet shall weep without relief
For ever bowed beneath a load of care;
The head and front of all who knighthood wear,
Richard the King is dead, the rich in heart.
Ah God! the loss, the pain, the bitter smart,
The woe! How strange, how wild a theme to sing!
Hard-hearted he who grieves not for the King.

Dead is he; and ten centuries' decay
Have never brought to earth so true a knight;
Ten centuries again shall pass away
Ere we see one so generous, bold and bright;
Darius' conqueror, Alexander's might,
Arthur nor Charlemagne could ne'er pretend
So freely of their bounty to dispend;
He was, in sooth, as all the world doth know,
Staunch to his friend, a terror to his foe.

A deeper note is struck in Giraut de Bornelh's *planh*[1]:

Er auch del rei qu'era plus pros
E plus valens en mans assais
De totz cels que vianda pais,
Que sobret mejas e maiors
E crec sos pretz e sas onors
E no temi' afan ni fais,
Que, si lo planhon dui,
Lo tertz lor o destrui,
Que · m par mal ensenhatz.
Qu'eu no cut c'ane fos natz,
De Charlemanh' en sai,
Reis per tan bel assai

[1] Kolsen, *G. de Bornelh*, Halle, 1910, p. 462, no. 73 (Si per mo Sobre-Totz no fos, quoted by Dante, *De V.E.*).

Mentaugutz ni prezatz;
Mas ja leu no crezatz
C'afars tan mal estei
Qu'ensems lo planhan trei!

E que val donc bela faissos
Ni grans poders c'aissi s'abais?
E ja passava part Roais
Lo noms e · l pretz e la paors
Entrels paias galiadors,
C'anc us sols plus arer no · ls trais!
Per que falh qui · s desdui,
Pos aissi leu s'esdui
So c'om plus vol ni · lh platz,
De que tenh per grevatz
Cels que mais podon sai,
Si non adoban lai,
Can chamjara rictatz,
C'aian cal que solatz
De lor gran charlabei
Denan lo maior rei.

"Now I hear of the King, who in many an enterprise was the best and bravest of all whom food doth feed, who surpassed high and low, who increased his fame and his possessions and did not shrink from toil and hardship, that if two lament his loss, a third disturbs it for them, and this seems to me ill teaching. For in my belief from Charles the Great until now, was never a king born who would be so praised and famed for such fair endeavours; but do not lightly believe that it would be so bad a thing that three should together lament him.

To what end, then, beauty of form and great power that thus are laid low? For indeed his name and fame and the terror of him among the treacherous heathen spread beyond Edessa; for no one has driven them further back. So it is wrong to nurse illusions, for what is loved and liked best, so easily passes away; therefore I consider those, who have most power in this world, to blame if they do not see to it, that, in the next world when their wealth is ended, they find before the Greatest King some recompense for their great splendour."

The Provençal *razo* to one of Arnaut Daniel's poems relates a well-known story, the historical truth of which cannot be controlled, but which illustrates the literary taste of the age. Arnaut Daniel while at Richard's court had a quarrel "with another joglar" on the question of their technical skill and wagered their respective palfreys on the issue. The king, who was stakeholder, shut them up in separate rooms until they had composed the poems which were to decide who was the better. Arnaut's invention failed him: but the rival sang his composition so loudly and continuously that Arnaut learnt it by heart, and on the day appointed for the decision he asked permission to begin and sang his opponent's song. The rival indignantly claimed his authorship, and when Arnaut confessed his trick the king was much amused, cancelled the wager and "a cascu fes donar bels dos."

Richard's military prowess became proverbial. Bertran d'Alamanon, referring to events in 1230, holds him up as a model:

> Aissi cum selh que a cor e talen
> De far los faitz que·l reis Richartz fazia[1].

He is coupled with his brothers Henry and Geoffrey as examples of knightly ideals; so Giraut de Calanson, in a *planh* on the death of Fernando, the

[1] Ed. Salverda de Grave, Toulouse, 1902, no. 1, l. 32.

son of Alfonso VIII of Castile and of Eleanor of England in 1211:

> Don cuiavon qu'en elh fos esmendatz
> Lo jove reys, e N'Richartz lo prezatz,
> E·l coms Jaufres, tug li trey valen fraire[1].

"Because of which men thought that in him were perfected the young king, the much-prized Richard and the Count Geoffrey, all the three valiant brothers."

Savaric de Mauleon is a troubadour who played a considerable part throughout John's reign. He was the son of Raoul of Mauleon (in North Poitou[2]), a baron who is once mentioned by Bertran de Born[3]; he was, according to his Provençal biography,

> a fair knight, courteous, learned and generous above all generous men. He was fonder than anyone in the world of the service of ladies, of love and tournaments, of song and composing songs...he was the best fighter that ever there was in the world.

That fanatical punster, Pierre des Vaux de Cernay, the historian of the Albigeois Crusade, gives another account of him in characteristic style:

> veniebat etiam...ille pessimus apostata, ille praevaricator iniquus, filius diaboli, minister Antichristi, Savaricus videlicet de Malleone, omnem excedens hereticum, omni deterior infideli, impugnator Ecclesiae, Christi hostis. O virum, immo virus pessimum, etc.[4]

[1] Mila, p. 125.

[2] Now Châtillon sur Sèvre. There is a Mauléon in the Basses Pyrénées and the lord of this place, also Savari, appears in the Querimonie Gastonis de Bearnis against Simon de Montfort when he was governor in Gascony 1248–54 (quoted by Bémont, *Simon de Montfort*, pp. 313–14). I know of no connection, and the identity of names appears to be a coincidence.

[3] Stimming, no. 5, l. 26.

[4] Quoted by Chabaneau, *Biog. des Troub.* p. 48. The historical

When John relieved the castle of Mirebeau in 1202, where Philip and Arthur of Brittany were besieging Queen Eleanor, he captured Savaric with other distinguished prisoners. According to the Provençal *razo* to a poem by Bertran de Born fils, Savaric was confined "*en la tor Corp*," where there was neither eating nor drinking, which Chabaneau identifies with Corfe Castle, in which Henry I had imprisoned his brother Robert. Savaric was liberated by John and became his zealous supporter. In 1204, he was in Poitou[1], helping John's seneschal, Robert of Turnham, against the Lusignans. Bertran de Born the younger refers to Philip's invasion of the English territory and the loss of Poitou and Touraine in a *sirventes* written apparently in the spring of 1205.

> Quan vei lo temps renovelar
> E pareis la fuolha e la flors,
> Mi dona ardimen amors
> E cor e saber de chantar;
> E puois vei qu'als no m'en sofranh,
> Farai un sirventes cozen,
> Que trametrai lai per presen
> A·l rei Johan, que·s n'avergonh.

notices concerning Savaric may be found in the indices of the *Historiens des Gaules et de la France*, tom. 17–21.

[1] To this period must belong a reference in MS. Harl. 311 (British Museum), Sim. d'Ewesii Collectanea, plerumque historica, fol. 130 *ro*: "Rex confirmavit Radulpho de Maleon et Willielmo de Maleon, et Savarico filio ejusdem Radolphi totum Talemondeis et les Mostiers des Mafels et Curson cum omnibus pertinentibus de Talemondeis per toto jure suo quod ipse et antecessores sui habuerunt in Rupella ac etiam rex concessit praefato Radulpho et Willielmo et Savarico decem milia solidorum monetae annuatim percipienda." The places mentioned are near La Rochelle in which the Mauleon family had held possessions.

E deuria · s be vergonhar,
Si · lh membres de sos ancessors.
Quar laissa sai Peitau e Tors
A · l rei Felip ses demandar;
Per que tota Guiana planh
Lo rei Richart que defenden
En mes maint aur e maint argen,
Mas d'aquest no · m par n'aia sonh.

"When I see the seasons renewed and the leaf and flower appear, love gives me boldness, heart and knowledge to sing; and as I see that I may not refrain from song, I will compose a bitter sirventes, which I will send there as a present to King John, that he may feel shame. Shame indeed he ought to feel, if he remembers his ancestors; for he abandons here Poitou and Tours to King Philip without even asking for them. So the whole of Guienne sorrows for King Richard, who expended so much gold and silver on its defence: but of that he does not seem so much as to dream."

In 1205 Savaric reconquered Niort by a stratagem, which, with La Rochelle, was the only fortress John held on the northern frontier of Poitou[1]; he subdued Gascony and was made seneschal of the province. To this period seems to refer a stanza in Peire Cardinal's *sirventes*, Aquesta gens...[2]

Que fan l'enfan d'aquella gen engleza,
qu'avan no van guerreiar ab Frances?
Mal an talan de la terr' engolmeza!
Tiran iran conquistar Gastines!
Ben sai que lai en Normandia
dechai e chai lor senhoria,
car los guarzos vezon en patz sezer.
Anctos es tos que trop pert per temer.

[1] R. Coggeshall, p. 146. Norgate, *John Lackland*, p. 113.

[2] Bartsch, *Gr.* Mahn, *W.* II, 214. For a discussion of the date, see K. Vossler, "Peire Cardinal," *Sitzungsberichte der königl. bayerischen Akademie*, München, 1916, p. 173.

"What are the sons of that English race doing, that they do not advance to war with France? Poor is their desire for the land of Angoulême! With delay they will proceed to conquer the Gâtinais! I know well that there in Normandy their rule sinks and falls, for they see the garrisons resting in peace. Shameful is he who loses much through fear."

About that time we may place his relations with the troubadour Uc de Saint-Circ, who appears to have been an intimate friend: in Savaric's biography he is said to have commissioned Uc to carry a letter to his lady, and Uc dedicated three of his poems to Savaric[1]. In 1211 he appears as himself seneschal of Poitou on the side of the Count of Toulouse in the Albigeois Crusade; in that year, his presence at the siege of Castelnaudari provoked the above quoted sketch of his character by Pierre des Vaux de Cernay. He turned against John in 1213 (possibly under papal influence), when the French king proposed to invade England to redress the wrongs of the Church and to punish John for the murder of Arthur[2]. In 1214, when John began

[1] *Uc de Saint-Circ*, Jeanroy et Salverda de Grave's ed., Toulouse, 1913, pp. 152–3.

[2] One of the few laudatory remarks passed upon John during the whole period was made by the troubadour Guillem Figueira, a bitter enemy of the Papacy and a declared friend of the Emperor Frederic II, whom he called his lord. In his long *sirventes* against Rome, he refers to the fact that John did homage to the Pope for his realm, in 1213 (Mahn, *Gedichte*, 140; Diez, *L. und W.* p. 455):

Car pretz e merces
Per vos mor e sosterra,
Roma enganairitz,
Q'etz de totz mals guitz
E cima e razitz,

his campaign in Poitou, Savaric submitted to him and secured a pardon by the intervention of the archbishop of Bordeaux. With Rainaut de Pons, another troubadour, he was a witness to the truce concluded between France and England in that year[1]. He supported John in 1215 during the Great Charter negotiations and the war between the king and the barons[2] and saved the garrison of Rochester, whom John wished to hang, by pointing out that the mercenaries, upon whom John relied, would refuse to serve in a war in which no quarter was given[3]. During John's winter harrying of the country, Savaric was with the army of the Eastern Counties. On Christmas Day he plundered Tilty Abbey during the celebration of Mass and repeated this sacrilege at Coggeshall on January 1, 1216. He joined in the attack upon Ely, when the garrison fled across the ice, and he was sent to

Q'el bons reis d'Englaterra
Fon per vos trahitz.

"For worth and desert by you are slain and buried, treacherous Rome, lodestar, crown and root of all evil, for the good King of England was by you betrayed."

John also had a troubadour ally in Robert, bishop of Clermont. See Stronski, *Ann. du Midi*, 1907, p. 550. Diez, *Leben u. Werke*, p. 95.

[1] Teulet, *Chartes*, I, 405, no. 1033.

[2] R. Wendover, III, 336.

[3] Collectanea ex rotulis in Archivis Turris Londoniensis, temp. Joh. et H. III. Harl. MS. British Museum, p. 48 (end of membrana 7a, a° 3° Reg. Joh.): "Savaricus de Malo Leone vicecomes Suthantonensis Testis vii° Junii, XVII° Regis. Et habuit castrum Portestrum (Porchester) custodiendum." John's 17th regnal year ran from May 28, 1215 to May 18, 1216—from one Ascension Day to the next: the reference may be to the safe conduct which he issued on Whitmonday, June 8, for the barons to go to and from Staines during the next three days.

attack Colchester, from which he retired on February 3, as relief from London was approaching. Surprised when reconnoitring ahead of the king's advance on London, Savaric was wounded and lost many of his men. When Louis invaded England Savaric was defending Winchester, the castle of which he evacuated on June 26 after burning half the town. In September John counter-attacked and overran the Eastern Counties; Savaric was then ordered to burn Croyland, but a procession of barefooted monks, with an image of the Virgin and other relics, supported by a bribe of 50 marks, induced him to spare the place: he was obliged to pacify the king's anger at this neglect of duty by destroying the year's crops which had been garnered in Croyland[1]. John gave him command of Lynn, which had opened its gates to the royal troops on October 9, and with some of the spoil from Croyland Savaric provisioned the town. He appears in John's will as one of his executors and was probably one of that grim funeral escort of foreign mercenaries which carried John's body from Newark to Worcester. After the death of John, he fought for Henry III in 1224 and defended Niort and La Rochelle in succession but lost both places for want of support. When the English cause in Poitou appeared hopeless, he went over to Louis, who treated him with marked distinction and gave him back his lands. In 1225 he fought for Louis against the Albigenses, whom he had before supported; but after that king's death he is again found on the

[1] M. Paris, *Hist. Angl.* II, 189–190.

side of England in Aquitaine, in 1227[1]. He died before November 27, 1231[2]. The only poetry of his which has come down to us consists of one stanza and his share in a *tenso*; but this is no proof of the extent of his literary production. In any case, he was one who may well have brought to England some taste and enthusiasm for the lyric poetry of his native land.

England took no official part in the Albigeois Crusade, which eventually scattered the troubadours far and wide, although Raimon VI, the Count of Toulouse and one of the chief sufferers, was connected with the English crown, as he had married in 1196 Jane, daughter of Henry II and sister of Richard Cœur de Lion. Jane, who was the fourth of Raimon's five wives, died in 1199, leaving a son, Raimon, afterwards the seventh Count of Toulouse, a daughter, and a son named Baudouin, who joined Simon de Montfort's side during the crusade and was captured and executed by his brother. Raimon VI attempted to secure the support of his brother-in-law, John[3], and went to England with

[1] He appears in that year with Jaufre Rudel de Blaya as guarantor of the truce concluded between Richard, brother of Henry III, Count of Poitou, and the King of France. Chabaneau, *loc. cit.*

[2] *Ann. du Midi*, XIII, year 1901, p. 530.

[3] Bernart Arnaut de Moncuc composed a *sirventes* in the spring of 1213, according to Diez, in which he satirised John for his dilatory and unwarlike attitude in failing to support Raimon, his brother-in-law (Diez, *L. und W.* p. 443. *Parnasse Occitanien*, p. 23):

Be · m plazo l'arquier
Pres la barbacana,
Quan trazo · l peirier
E · l mur dezenvana;
E per mant verdier
Creis la ost e gensa.

his son for this purpose in 1215, returning to the Continent in time to be present at the fourth Lateran council[1]. John had other matters to occupy his mind at that moment. Raimon is said by Raoul de Coggeshale to have done homage to John and to have surrendered to him the city of Toulouse, in return for which John gave him 10,000 silver marks. John sent the abbot of Beaulieu (Bewley, New Forest, Hants) to the council and the *Chanson de la Croisade* represents him as speaking on behalf of Raimon; but his chief business was to put John's case in his quarrel with Stephen Langton, the archbishop of Canterbury. These facts, apart from the English connections of Simon de Montfort, show that communication between England and the south of France was continual.

The Monk of Montaudon refers to John's relations with the emperor Otto IV, in a stanza which has come to us in isolation[2]:

> Seigner, s'agessetz regnat
> Per conseill dels vostres baillos,
> No·us mandara·l reis N'Anfos
> Tant salut, ni tant amistat,
> Ni no·us agra tant onrat

> E volgra·l plagues
> Aital captenensa
> Lai al rei Engles.

"Very pleasing to me are the archers near the barbican when the mangonels fire and the wall collapses and through many a garden advances the host in array. And I would that the English king had as much delight in it."

[1] G. de Puylaurens, ch. 25: "interfuerunt comes et filius ejus Tolosanus, qui de Anglia venit cum quodam mercatore." So the *Chanson de la Croisade*, 3170 ff.

[2] Philippson, *Der Mönch von Montaudon*, Halle a. S. 1873, p. 55.

Chai, Proenza ni tota Lumbardia,
Ni, a Nicart, non agra seignoria
Lo reis Joanz plus que a Saint-Massenz
Se regnassetz per conseill de servenz.

"Sir, if you had reigned according to the advice of your officials, King Alfonso would not send you so earnest and friendly a greeting, nor on this side would Provence and Lombardy have so honoured you: nor, at Newark, would King John have any more power than he has at Saint Maixent, if you were to reign as your servants wish."

By the end of 1209, Otto had been generally recognised as emperor after the assassination of his Ghibelline rival, Philip of Hohenstaufen; Alfonso VIII of Castile, who had married Eleanor of England[1] and was his uncle, sent him a friendly message. The Pope thought of inducing him to lead a new crusade. He was the uncle of John and supported him in his quarrel with the English clergy by his influence at Rome. The Monk, as a famous troubadour, may well have known Otto, when Richard Cœur de Lion, his uncle, brought him up at his court in Aquitaine. Richard had shown much affection for his sister Matilda's son and had secured his election as emperor in 1198. The officials against whose advice Otto acted were, no doubt, the ecclesiastical dignitaries with whom he was always struggling, and the Monk probably wrote his poem about 1212 when both John and Otto were most deeply involved in their struggle with the Church powers. The situa-

[1] On the death of her son Fernando, 1211, the troubadour Giraut de Calanson composed a *planh* which refers to grief in England and France. Mila, p. 125.

tion was completely changed by the battle of Bouvines in 1214[1].

Innocent III issued an appeal for a crusade in the spring of 1213 and an unknown troubadour invited John to take part in it:

> Al rei Felip et a · n Oto
> et al rei Joan eisamen
> laus que fasson acordamen
> entr'els e segon lo perdo,
> e servon a sancta Maria,
> don sos fils pert la senhoria
> de Suria del comte de
> Sur tro al renhe d'Egipte[2].

"I would that King Philip and Sir Otto and King John made agreement together and served St Mary whose Son loses His lordship of the province of Syria from Tyre to the realm of Egypt."

The Pope's attempts were fruitless.

One of Henry III's favourite projects was the recovery of the lost territories in France. To this

[1] This is the interpretation of M. Fabre, *Ann. du Midi*, year 1908, p. 351. The only objection to it is the profession of the Monk who produced these anti-Church sentiments: but he cannot be described as a strong churchman, upon other grounds. Newark was the castle in which John died and a favourite residence: Saint Maixent is for Poitou, which John lost to Philippe Auguste in 1209. To refer to countries and provinces in this way is quite in the style of the Monk: in no. 12 of Philippson's ed., he thus refers to Richard (who had then just been liberated): "ben mal o fezis / que tost non anes coichos / al rei cui es Olairos / qui tant era tos amics." "You did very wrong in not going at once to the king who holds Oléron, who was so much your friend." Oléron is an island at the mouth of the Charente. Fabre is probably right in regarding the stanza as part of a longer poem and not as a *cobla esparsa*.

[2] Zenker, *Peire von Auvergne*, p. 147.

attempt he was urged by the troubadour Amoros dau Luc[1]:

> Ai reis Engles! Non siaz flac ni vans,
> qe ges aissi la Rochela n'er prisa.

"O, English king, be not feeble and vain, for never thus will La Rochelle be captured,"

which Louis IX had captured on August 3, 1224. In 1230 he made an unsuccessful attempt to recover Brittany; in 1238 he sent troops to Italy[2] to help the emperor Frederic II who had married his sister Isabella, and was then at war with Milan. The troubadour Uc de Saint-Circ gives a promise by Frederic as the inducement for this dispatch of troops, but whether it was actually made cannot be confirmed from other evidence.

> Lo falcos, filh de l'aigla, quez es reys dels Frances,
> Sapcha que Fredericx a promes als Engles
> Qu'el lor rendra Bretanha, Anjou et Toarces,
> E Peytau e Sayntonge, Lemotges, Engolmes,
> Toroinn'e Normandia e Guiana e·l Paes,
> E·n venjara Tolzan, Bezers e Carcasses[3].

"Let the falcon, the son of the eagle, who is King of France, know that Frederic has promised to the English that he will restore to them Brittany, Anjou and the

[1] O. Schultz-Gora, *Prov. Studien*, II, Berlin and Leipzig, 1921, p. 123.

[2] Matthew Paris, *Hist. Angl.* 1st ed. Lond. 1571, p. 413 (quoted by Zingarelli).

[3] Zingarelli, *Intorno a due trovatori in Italia*, Florence, 1899, pp. 8 ff.; *Poésies de Uc de Saint-Circ*, Jeanroy et Salverda de Grave, Toulouse, 1913, no. 23. The "Paes" is not the pays de Chartres, as Z. states: J. and S. de G. suggest one of the numerous "pays" in Upper Normandy, or that the word applies to the whole of the regions seized by France and sums up all that are named separately.

district of Thouars, Poitou and Saintonges, Limoges and Angoulême, the Touraine and Normandy, Guienne and the 'Pays' and that he will avenge the district of Toulouse, Béziers and the country of Carcassonne."

Probably to Henry III is also to be referred a mutilated stanza from a *sirventes* by Guillem Anelier of Toulouse:

> quar lo reys ditz
> Joves Engles, quez ab colps et ab critz
> Volra cobrar tot quant tenc ses falhida
> Lo pros Richartz, oy er testa partida[1].

"For the king, the young Englishman says that with blows and war-cries he will recover without fail all that the brave Richard held or a head will be split."

Provençal influence at the English court increased considerably during the reign of Henry III; after the fall of his justiciar, Hubert de Burgh, natives of Poitou found a useful patron in Peter des Roches. Henry's marriage with Eleanor of Provence[2] in

[1] Ed. by Gisi (Solothurn, 1877), no. 3. Tobler referred the allusion to Edward I.

[2] She was the second daughter of Raimon Berenguer IV (1209–45). For the story of the Romieu (Dante, *Par.* VI, 135) and his success in marrying the count's daughters to kings, see references in Chabaneau and Anglade's edition of Jehan de Nostredame, Paris, 1913. Matthew Paris, *Angl. Hist.* p. 406, says of the wedding feast, "Quid in mensa dapium et diversorum libaminum describam fertilitatem redundantem, venationis abundantiam, piscium varietatem, *joculatorum voluptatem*?" Nostradamus says that Eleanor was the author of the narrative poem in Provençal, *Blandin de Cornouailles*; see Anglade's ed. of Nostr. p. 86. In Henry's service was one Richard le Harpeur (see *Les Savoyards en Angleterre*, F. Mugnier, Chambéry, 1890, p. 208). This person appears more than once in the Gascon Rolls: in 1242 (Bémont's ed. vol. I, no. 149), "Mandatum est Hugoni Giffarde quod retineat Ricardum le Harpur ad solacium puerorum et ei necessaria sua inveniat." The boys in question were

1236 was the signal for numbers of Provençals to make their way to England, under the protection of Eleanor's uncles, William of Valence, Boniface and Peter of Savoy[1]. His own brother Richard had been insulted by the nomination of Alfonso as Count of Poitou, a title belonging to the Plantagenets and the affront was deeply resented in England.

Henry's mother, Isabella of Angoulême, had married Hugh de la Marche and Henry's half-brothers also appeared in England to push their fortunes. In 1242 she induced Henry to send an expedition to Gascony in support of his step-father, whom she had persuaded to revolt against the King of France. This expedition was part of a great attempt made by the south of France to recover its independence, the leading spirit being Raimon of Toulouse, who wished to destroy the treaty of 1229, by which, on his death, all his possessions were to pass, with the hand of his only daughter Jeanne, to a brother of the French king. The several princes had made an alliance against the young King of

Prince Edward and the eldest son of Nicolas de Molis, a Gascon who was brought up with him. In 1255 (no. 3508) the king ordered fur cloaks and other apparel to be given to Richard and his wife. There is no evidence that Richard was a Gascon, but we need not conclude with Bémont that he was a Welshman because he played the harp. The *istriones* referred to in the Gascon Rolls (2935, 3328, 3384) are as likely to have been court jesters as professional musicians.

[1] If instances are required, Henry forced the Chapter of Winchester to elect his half-brother, Aimar de Valence, as bishop in 1250. Similarly, he made Pierre d'Aigueblanche, a Provençal, bishop of Hereford.

France and much was hoped from the adherence of England. Henry III set sail for France on May 9, 1241, and about this time appeared a fiery *sirventes* by Peire del Vilar[1]:

> Pecs er si ses pro companhos
> Se pleja de las flors triar.
> Pero si ben vol anparar
> Lo castel, l'ala ni · l bastos,
> Passar pot Escots et Engles,
> Noroecx et Irlans e Gales:
> Mas tart n'aura · il flor de ver senh
> Si de larc despendre s'estrenh.
>
> E si · l plai bella messios,
> Gen prometre, largamen dar,
> Semblara del linhatge car
> Don foro · ls fraires valoros,
> N'Anrics, en Richartz, en Jofres;
> E poira cobra Guianes
> E Normandia; don me senh
> Car plus tost non troba mantenh.

"It will be a sin if without his stout comrades he should please himself with weaving flowers. But if he wishes to seize the castle, the outworks and the bastions, he can bring Scotch and English, Norwegians, Irish and Welsh: but he will hardly get the flower set in green, if he is niggardly in his expenditure.

And if fair outlay pleases him, fair promises and generous giving, he will seem to be of that dear line whence were the valorous brothers, Henry, Richard and Geoffrey: and he will be able to recover Guienne and Normandy; for which I yearn, for ere that I find no support."

The English were beaten at Saintes on July 23

[1] Jeanroy, "Le soulèvement de 1243," *Ann. du Midi*, year 1904, and in "Mélanges Léonce Couture," *Études d'histoire méridionale*, Toulouse, 1902, pp. 115–125.

and Louis IX then defeated the barons of Poitou in detail. The alliance collapsed: Raimon VII of Toulouse had succeeded in raising a force in Languedoc but he wasted time in futile negotiations, until he had secured a new alliance with Henry III (August 28—September 3), when the sudden defection of the Count of Foix (October 5) ruined his prospects, and the kings of Aragon and Castile, his most powerful allies, held aloof from so doubtful an enterprise. He had to submit on October 20. To these October days belongs the *sirventes* of Guilhem Montanhagol, who pours scorn upon the King of Aragon, and the Counts of La Marche and of Foix, praises Raimon and mocks at the inactivity of the English army, which, he seems to think, might yet turn the scale:

Engles, de flor
Faitz capel e de fuelha;
No · us detz trebalh,
Neis qui · us assalh
Tro qu'om tot vos o tuelha[1].

"English, crown yourselves with flowers and leaves; do not trouble, even if you are attacked, until they despoil you of your all."

The English king abandoned the attempt in 1243 (April 7) and the only tangible result was a further influx of foreigners who returned to England with the expedition. The bitter disappointment of the defeated parties is expressed in a *sirventes* by Duran, the tailor of Pernes (or Carpentras)[2]:

[1] Ed. Coulet, *Bibl. Méridionale*, p. 76.

[2] Jeanroy, *loc. cit.* I have followed his account, and his arguments for the date of this *sirventes* seem absolutely decisive.

En talent hai q'un sirventes encoc
Per traire a cels q'an mes Pretz a deroc,
Qar mantenon "No" e han faidit "Hoc":
E menz q'ieu ai arbalesta e croc,
Brocarai lai per traire al major loc,
Al rei emgleis, qes hom ten per badoc,
Qar suefr' aunitz q'om del sieu lo descoc;
Per q'en cor ai qe als primiers lo toc.

"I wish to fit a *sirventes* to the bowstring to shoot those who have laid Honour low, for they favour No and have banished Yes; as long as I have an arblast and rest, I will spur (my horse) to shoot at the highest place, at the English king who is considered a fool; for in his dishonour he allows men to spoil him of his goods; and therefore I wish him to be struck first."

Then follows a stanza upon the King of Aragon. Other cases occur where troubadours couple these kings for reproach or for exhortation. Paulet de Marseille (see p. 95) hopes for an alliance between their children. "Either the troubadours themselves believed that only the union of these two great states could make head against the Capetian monarchy, or the succession of such appeals was inspired by a word of command[1]," sent round the troubadours and jongleurs of reputation. Similar "press campaigns" are not unknown in modern times.

Bernart de Rovenac, apparently in the second half of the year 1241, said[2]:

Rey Engles prec que entenda,
Quar fa dechazer

[1] Jeanroy, *loc. cit.*

[2] Jeanroy, *loc. cit.* Mila, p. 178. *Romanische Forschungen*, vol. XXII, 1908; G. Bosdorff, *Bernard von Rovenac*, p. 768.

Son pauc pretz per trop temer,
Quar no · l play que · ls sieus defenda;
Qu'ans es tan flacx e marritz
Que par sia adurmitz,
Qu'elh reys franses li tolh en plas perdos
Tors et Angieus e Normans e Bretos.

"I pray that the English king may hear me, since by his extreme cowardice he reduces his small prestige, for it does not please him to defend his own property; on the contrary, he is so feeble and poor-spirited that he seems to be asleep, while the King of France utterly deprives him of Tours, Anjou, Normandy and Brittany."

The next stanza alludes to the King of Aragon in similar terms. The English claims to the provinces mentioned were finally relinquished in 1259 under the treaty of Paris, in return for the cession of territory in the south of France. The famous *planh* of Sordello refers to these two kings in successive stanzas[1]:

Del Rey engles me platz, quar es pauc coratjos,
Que manje pro del cor, pueys er valens e bos,
E cobrara la terra, per que viu de pretz blos,
Que · l tol lo Reys de Fransa quar lo sap nualhos.

"For the King of England it pleases me, as he is lacking in courage, that he should eat much of the heart, and then he will be brave and good and will recover the land, for which he lives devoid of honour, which the King of France took from him, because he knew him to be of no account."

The King of Aragon is to eat of the heart that he may lose the disgrace which he incurred by

[1] De Lollis, *Sordello*, Rom. Bibliothek, v, p. 154. Bertoni, *Trov. d'Italia*, p. 286. On the date, see Fabre, *Ann. du Midi*, XXIV (year 1912), pp. 180 ff., who regards it as composed in 1242, while Salverda de Grave (*ibid.* p. 561) prefers an earlier date.

failing to make good his claims upon Marseilles and Milhau: the former might have been his upon the death of his cousin Raimon Berenger without male issue and the latter, an old fief of the house of Aragon, remained in the hands of Raimon VII of Toulouse with the consent of Louis IX and the Pope.

Henry's fondness for foreign favourites aroused general exasperation which contributed to the success of Simon de Montfort's rebellion: this uprising put an end to the importation of foreigners. De Montfort was the second son of the leader of the crusade against the Albigenses and had married Henry's sister, Eleanor; from 1248 to 1254 he had been governor of Gascony[1].

Bernart de Rovenac early in 1254[2] refers to the absence of St Louis on the sixth crusade and states that the kings of Aragon and England had agreed not to take advantage of his absence:

> Amdos los reis an una cauz' empresa
> Selh d'Arago et aisselh dels Engles,
> Que no sia per elhs terra defesa,
> Ni fasson mal ad home que·l lur fes;

[1] The severity with which he maintained his authority produced numerous complaints, and in 1252 a deputation of Gascons came to London to put their case in person. Some of these documents of grievances, in Latin and Provençal, are printed by Bémont, *Simon de Montfort*, Appendix, nos. 13–28.

[2] *Rom. Forsch.*, *loc. cit.* p. 799. Henry III had more than once promised to join a crusade and had done nothing: he accepted the throne of Sicily for his son Edmund, because he thought that if he fought against the excommunicated Manfred who had seized the crown and against the African Saracens who were numerous in the island, he might thus satisfy his conscience and perhaps the Pope.

E fan merce e cortesia
Quar al re que conquer Suria
Laisson en patz lor fieus del tot tener;
Nostre Senher lor en deu grat saber.

"Both kings of Aragon and England have undertaken one purpose, that no land shall be devastated by them, and that they will do no harm to the man who harmed them; and they show him kindness and courtesy, for they allow the king to hold their fiefs in peace, that he may conquer Syria: our Lord should show them favour for it."

This eulogy is probably ironical; Henry, at any rate, was in no position to attack France at this time.

About the same time Bonifacio III of Castellana[1]

[1] Appel, *Prov. Ined.* p. 83. Mila, p. 176. Mila's date, 1241, is impossible, in view of other allusions in the *sirventes*. Appel dates it 1250–54. Salverda de Grave, *Bertran d'Alamanon*, p. 59, proposes 1259. The question is to find which historical situation will best explain the allusions in the poem, and the best stanza to examine first is no. 5.

E li fals clerge renegat
cuidan deseretar Colrat
per donar a lor bastardos,
e tenon l'emperi vacat
ab las lur malvaisas lesos,
don cuian reinhar entre nos;
mas San Peir han trop irascut.

"And the false renegade clergy think to disinherit Conradin to endow their bastard and they keep the empire vacant with their malignant reasonings, by which they think to reign among us; but they have angered St Peter too deeply." Conrad IV, the emperor, died in May 1254, leaving Conradin, aged two, as his heir in Sicily, under the regency of the Margrave Berthold of Hohenburg; Manfred, the bastard son of the late emperor, Frederic II, succeeded in turning out Berthold and securing the regency for himself. But Pope Innocent IV attacked him, Berthold joined the Pope and Manfred was obliged to agree to a peace in September 1254. Innocent intended to see a candidate of his own choice on the Sicilian throne and had already sounded Richard of Cornwall and Edmund of England. The troubadour regards the attempt to

gives his opinion of Henry III and of the King of Aragon in successive stanzas:

> Lo rei engles cug q'a·l sanglut,
> qar tan lo ve hom estar mut
> de demandar sas eretatz;
> e mentr' est autr' han tan perdut,
> degra si menar daus totz latz
> coredors e cavals armatz,
> tro cobres sas possessios.

"I think that the English king has hiccups (death-rattle), for he is seen so dumb to demand his inheritance; and while the others have lost everything, he should bring up in all directions runners and armed chargers until he recovers his possessions."

Jaime of Aragon is then reproached for wasting in negotiations opportunities for war.

In 1256 the death of William of Holland made an election of a German emperor necessary. The German Guelfs and the Hohenstaufen party saw

disregard Conradin as due to the long-standing hatred of Germans and South Italians fostered by the clergy for their own purposes. As to the empire, the Great Interregnum had existed in reality for four years, and the death of Conrad made the question even more pressing. If there were no emperor, the Church would be supreme; hence the last line but one of the stanza.

To return to stanza 3, that referring to Henry III quoted above, the chief difficulty is the fourth line; who were the others who have lost everything? Appel explains the line as possibly an allusion to the disasters of the sixth crusade in Egypt, from which Louis had returned in June 1254. The plural may include the nobles who had joined Louis in this adventure, such as Alfonso of Poitiers and Robert of Artois; all were weakened by the huge losses and expenses of the crusade and the troubadour therefore urged Henry III to seize so favourable an opportunity as the moment of the king's return. To have attacked in his absence would have been to incur the wrath of the Church.

that a compromise was the only means of settling their quarrels and looked about for a candidate who would be acceptable to the Pope and friendly to Suabian interests. Richard, Earl of Cornwall, was a good friend of the Pope and had also been a brother-in-law and ally of Frederic II, while his wealth enabled him to secure support. But the Italian Ghibellines wanted an emperor who would favour their ancient feuds and France thought England already more than sufficiently powerful. They therefore supported the candidature of Alfonso IX of Castile. The troubadour Folquet de Lunel supported the Spanish candidate, as also did Raimon de Tors de Marseilla, in the following *sirventes*[1]:

1 Ar es dretz q'ieu chan e parlle,
Pos de Viena e d'Arlle
Vol esser reis En Richartz,
Don ha dol le Reis de Karlle
E ric plazer N'Odoartz
Qe non es lotz ni coartz.

2 Per q'ieu mon chantar esmeri,
Qar cuia aver l'emperi
E seinhorezar Lonbartz
Qi sabon tot lo sauteri
De cor e totas las partz
E mais qe per las VII artz.

3 E qar le reis de Castella,
Qe prez e valor capdella,
Estan ab sos Espainhols
Vol l'emperi ni l'apella,

[1] Mila, p. 214. Mahn, *Gedichte*, 324. No corrections have been made on Mahn's copy of M. Mila reads glotz in l. 6.

Don ieu dic q'ez escurols
Non es plus lieus que sos vols.

4 Quar es de prez emperaires,
E de valor caps et paires,
E fins jois es sos filhos,
E fin amors es sa maires,
E gais solatz sos estolls,
E sos grans enemics dols.

5 E qar sai q'a nostre comte
De Proensa rendra comte
Qi · s coronera lonc clau,
Mas ja ieu los colps non conte,
Q'ez en massis ez en cau
Si ferran fort e suau.

6 Qan la corona de ferre
Venran clerc ez Engles qerre
L'un ab força e l'autr' ab frau,
Pero qals qe s'en sotzterre,
Clerg en faran a dieu lau
En vistran vermeilh e blau.

1. "Now it is right for me to sing and speak, since Sir Richard would be King of Vienne and Arles, for which King Charles is grieved and Sir Edward richly pleased, who is not slothful or cowardly."

2. "Wherefore I sing my best, since he wishes to have the empire and to domineer over the Lombards, who know the whole Psalter by heart and every part of it, and better than by means of the seven arts (i.e. than if they had been through the Trivium and Quadrivium)."

3. "And (I sing) since the King of Castile, whom worth and valour guide among his Spaniards, desires and claims the empire, of whom I say that the squirrel is not swifter than his movements."

4. "For he is emperor of worth, the head and father of excellence and pure joy is his son and pure love his mother and bright pleasure his escort and sorrow his great enemy."

5. "Indeed I know that he who is crowned will for long (?) have a score to settle with our Count of Provence, but I do not count the blows which both openly and in secret will be struck hard and quietly."

6. "When the Clerk and the Englishman come to seek the iron crown, the one with force and the other with fraud, whichever of the two succumbs, the clergy will utter praise to God robed in red and blue."

After the battle of Evesham, the country was so far pacified that Edward was able to join the last great crusade in 1270, for which Louis IX had been preparing since 1267. The troubadour Gauceran de Saint Leidier was confiding enough to suggest that Henry should join this crusade:

> Per qu'ieu volgra clergues prezicadors
> Fosson part Sur ea outra mar passatz,
> E · l reys engles e sos fraires Richartz
> E · l reys valens de cui es Aragos,
> Selh de Fransa, e · l princeps ab sa gen.

"I would that the preaching clergy would cross the sea to Tyre, and the English king with his brother Richard and the valiant King of Aragon and the King of France and the prince with his men[1]."

Richard is specially mentioned here on account of the enterprise he had previously shown, and also because he was now emperor. The king of Aragon was Jaime I. The prince is thought by Diez to be Henry's son, afterwards Edward I, who is thus

[1] Mahn, *Werke*, II, p. 44. K. Lewent, *Das altprovenzalische Kreuzlied*, p. 39. Diez, *L. u. W.* p. 268.

mentioned apart from his father in consequence of the special position and reputation he had gained by his victory over the Earl of Leicester.

Edward had married Eleanor of Castile, the sister of Alfonso the Wise, an arrangement which put an end to Alfonso's project of an expedition to recover Gascony, which had passed to England by Henry II's marriage with Eleanor of Aquitaine. The troubadour Bonifacio Calvo had supported the demand made by the Counts of Béarn and Gascony for help in a rising against the English, but his bellicose *sirventes* met with no response from Alfonso. The severity of de Montfort's rule as seneschal of Gascony from 1248 to 1252 no doubt aroused much popular unrest which was allayed when Edward was invested with all the king's dominions overseas[1]. The Italian troubadour Percivalle Doria[2] alludes to these events:

Mas Engles si van vanan
    Q'ill venran
E l'Emperi enqerran.
En Espagn' a pro d'afan,
Qe · il Serrazi no · il rendran
Per lur Granada ugan.

"But the English are boasting that they will come and claim the empire. In Spain there is trouble enough, because the Saracens will not surrender Granada this year."

[1] This was the remedy desired by the Gascons themselves. One of their petitions asks the king "quod amoveatis comitem...et mittatis filium vestrum dominum Edwardum dominum nostrum, in adventu quorum (*sic*) omnia erunt in pace, si vos ire nolletis." Bémont, *Simon de Montfort*, p. 312.

[2] Bertoni, *Trov. d'Italia*, no. 31.

The Church favoured this investiture and the Italian Guelfs hoped that the English would gain by force of arms what they thought to be their rights. The troubadour Austorc de Segret in a *planh*[1] upon the death of St Louis, written between 1270 and 1274, refers to the problems before Edward:

> A aura ops proez' et ardimens
> a·n Audoart, si vol Haenric veniar,
> qu'era de sen et de saber ses par
> e totz lo mielhs era de sos parens;
> e, si reman aras d'aisso aunitz,
> no·l laissaran ni cima ni razitz
> frances de sai, ni forsa ben garnida,
> si sa valors es de pretz desgarnida.

"Now to Sir Edward will be need of prowess and bravery, if he wishes to avenge Henry who was without peer in sense and knowledge and the best of all his family; and if he henceforward remains as dishonoured, the French here will leave him neither top nor root, nor well found fortress, if his worth is void of value."

Appel's edition has Na Enric (against the MS.) which the editor refers, apparently ironically, to Henry III, whose feminine weakness Edward is to "avenge" by recovering his lost possessions. This is distinctly far-fetched and Fabre has given a better explanation of the allusion: valueless as troubadour estimates of character sometimes are, Henry III could not be described, by any stretch of imagination, as the "best of Edward's family"; further Charles of Anjou is the man upon whom vengeance is desired, as the following stanza shows:

[1] Appel, *Prov. Ined.* p. 15. C. Fabre, *Ann. du Midi*, XXII (1910), p. 467.

> Guerras mortals veirem leu e sanglens,
> Que fora mals si pogues escapar
> Guis, e'N Karles no conogues son bar.
> Yeu, ses temor et ab descauzimens,
> Volgra vezer e cazer los marritz,
> E derrocar fortz castelhs ben bastitz,
> E qu'om crides soven, "A la guerida!"
> A N·Audoart qu'a la patz envazida[1].

"Soon shall we see deadly and bloody war, for it would be ill if Guy (de Montfort) could escape punishment and if Charles should not acknowledge his master. I, without fear and in their dishonour, would like to see both the downfall of the wretches and the overthrow of strong well-built castles and to hear men continually cry 'Help!' to Sir Edward, for he has broken the peace."

The Henry in question is Henry of Germany, the eldest son of Richard of Cornwall and Edward's cousin. He had helped to defeat Simon de Montfort at Evesham and had then gone to Italy to represent his father's rights at the papal court at Viterbo, a matter of importance to him, as his father had nominated him as his successor. His diplomacy was successful, and he then went to Tunis to follow his cousin Edward upon the crusade of 1270. Charles of Anjou had persuaded Louis to disembark at Tunis, in the interests of the house of Anjou and its Sicilian possessions; on the death of Louis, Charles and the new king, Philip the Bold, abandoned the crusade and returned to France. Henry followed them, at his cousin's request, to protect Guienne from possible French attacks. All three

[1] This stanza has been badly mutilated in the MS. and is thus ingeniously reconstructed by Fabre.

halted at Viterbo, to be present at the election of a new Pope: the death of Clement IV at the end of 1268 called for further diplomacy from Henry, while Philip and Charles naturally wanted a French Pope. Guy de Montfort was then at Viterbo, as he was the son-in-law of the Count of Tuscany, Aldobrandini Rosso. He, with French approval, proposed to assassinate Henry, in revenge for Henry's share in the death of his father, Simon de Montfort, at Evesham. Henry was aware of this design and was careful to wear the inviolable dress of a crusader. The precaution was useless: Guy stabbed him in church at the moment of the elevation of the Host and took refuge with his father-in-law; Richard of Cornwall, on hearing that his son had been thus atrociously murdered, was stricken with apoplexy and died on April 2, 1271, a short time after the murder was committed. Nothing was done until Edward returned in the spring of 1273, when the new Pope, Gregory X, excommunicated Guy, and allowed him eventually to reside in a fortress within papal territory under the guardianship of Charles of Anjou, with whom he could not afford to quarrel. This was apparently the most that Edward could secure as punishment for the murderer,

> Colui fesse in grembo a Dio
> Lo cuor che'n sul Tamigi ancor si cola[1].

Austorc de Segret thus wrote his *sirventes* between 1270 and 1273.

[1] Dante, *Inferno*, XII, 10 (quoted by Fabre).

In 1280 Edward was concerned in the affairs of Alfonso X of Castile. During the absence of the latter in France in 1277 his second son, Don Sancho, had declared himself heir to the throne, setting aside the claims of the sons of Ferdinand de la Cerda, the king's eldest brother. Alfonso decided to recognise this step and the infantes de la Cerda, under the protection of their grandmother, Doña Violante, fled for refuge to their great-uncle, Pedro III of Aragon. Doña Violante also brought their mother to Pedro's court: she was Blanche, the sister of Philip the Bold of France. Philip threatened to invade Castile, but was dissuaded by the Pope, who was supported by Edward, the brother-in-law of Alfonso. His efforts were successful and on November 26, 1280, Alfonso signed a treaty with the King of France at Seville. The event is noted with satisfaction by the troubadour Guiraut Riquier[1]:

> Plazer deu al rey Engles
> Lurs acortz, quar sospeyssos
> Non l'an, e plagra · m que y fos
> Elh e · l reys Aragones.

"Their agreement should please the English king, for they have confidence in him and I should like him and the King of Aragon to be there."

Paulet of Marseilles in a *pastorela* (which may be incorrectly attributed to him) makes the shepherdess talk politics, a most unusual proceeding in this poetical *genre*. She complains of the oppression

[1] Mahn, *Werke*, IV, p. 51. Anglade, *Guiraut Riquier*, p. 166.

of Charles of Anjou and hopes that Pedro of Aragon will come and claim the former possessions of his family, i.e. Provence. She then hopes that Pedro and Edward of England will join forces, and the poet also wishes that these two princes may "begin a game in which many helmets will be shattered and corslets stripped."

> Senher, ieu volgra de N'Audoart
> E del nobl' enfan ferm amor,
> Pos cascuns ha bel cors galhart,
> E que ama pretz e valor[1].

"Sir, I shall wish firm love in the case of Sir Edward and the noble infant, since each of them has a fine bold person and loves worth and valour."

The infant, the son of Jaime I, had succeeded his father as Pedro III; his claim to Provence came from Alfonso II of Aragon, who held it in 1167 as husband of Douce of Provence, the daughter of Raimon Berenger. Edward was interested for similar reasons, as the following will show:

Provence		*Aragon*
1167–8	Alfonso II	1162–96
Raimon Berenger III, 1168–81	brothers of Alfonso	Pedro II, son of Alfonso, 1196–1213
Sancho, 1181–85		|
Alfonso III, son of Alfonso, 1185–1209		Jaime I, 1213–76
|		|
Raimon Berenger IV, 1209–45		Pedro III, 1276–85

Edward's mother was Eleanor, daughter of Raimon

[1] *Le troubadour Paulet de Marseille*, E. Lévy, Paris, 1882, no. 8, and introduction.

Berenger IV. The poem was written, as an allusion shows, between 1265 and 1266.

So much will suffice to show the continued interest in English affairs which the troubadours displayed to the end of the 13th century. It remains to explain in what respects their influence is perceptible in Middle English literature.

III

TROUBADOUR INFLUENCE UPON THE ENGLISH LYRIC

MIDDLE English lyric poetry and its later developments were strongly influenced by mediaeval Latin poetry and by Provençal lyric poetry, the latter working through the medium of northern French imitations or possibly directly. The chief points of technique in which imitation is apparent are the construction of the stanza and the distribution of its rimes. A Teutonic metrical system could not attempt to reproduce the outstanding feature of Romance systems, identity in the number of syllables which compose two corresponding lines. Teutonic metrical regularity is secured by the regular recurrence of accented syllables. Romance languages, generally speaking, regard the syllable and not the group of syllables as the unit. Hence the metrical irregularities found in Anglo-Norman poetry are due to the fact that an ear accustomed to an accentual system of metre was attempting to accommodate itself to a syllabic system; such irregularities would vary with the idiosyncrasies of the writer and attempts to discover some general rule to account for these variations are hopeless. There is, therefore, nothing to be gained by attempting to compare the single line in English and French or

Provençal poems: the fundamental metrical differences make comparison impossible.

By rime we mean identity, in any two words, of the tonic vowel and of all sounds following this vowel. Anglo-Saxon poetry used rime in this sense, but not as an element of stanza construction. Alliteration, which is so prominent a feature in Middle English poetry, was affected by a few troubadours[1]—Peire d'Alvernhe and Peire Cardinal in particular—but there is no evidence to show any action or reaction between English and Romance poetry in this respect. It need hardly be said that the distribution of the rimes which unite several lines to form a stanza, must be the same in all subsequent stanzas as in the first. English is poor in rimes compared with Provençal or French; yet poets successfully attempted the more complicated and artistic stanza-forms which southern France produced. Nor was it possible to follow the strict practice of the classical troubadours, which allowed a close vowel to rime only with a close vowel and an open vowel only with an open. The use of identical rimes throughout all the stanzas of a poem, helped by the Romance use of "equivocal" rime, was also impossible for English resources, except as a *tour de force*, though stanzas upon a single set of rimes occur. Middle English poets occasionally repeat the last rime of one stanza at the beginning of the next stanza (Laurence Minot), this rime also answering another within each respective stanza;

[1] M. Scholz, "Die Alliteration in der prov. Lyrik," *Zeitschrift für rom. Phil.* vol. 37 (1913), p. 418.

as far as it goes, this use follows the Provençal *canso redonda*, in which the second stanza repeated the rimes of the first in inverse order. A commoner means of "concatenation" in Middle English poetry is the use of refrain (known as the "burden"). This was known to the Provençals as *refrim*, but occurs only in poems of popular origin, of which few examples survive.

The Middle English stanza follows the rules for stanza construction as formulated by Dante in his *De Vulgari Eloquentia*. These rules depend upon the primary fact that Provençal lyrics were intended to be sung and that the majority of poets were also composers. The musical setting was regarded as the composer's property, since it implied a special stanza construction, and acknowledgement was generally made if another poet borrowed it. This musical setting, upon which the form of the stanza depended, might be continuous without repetition or division; or it might be repeated, in which case the stanza was also divided into two parts, Dante's term for the division being *diesis* or *volta*. Of these two parts, either or both might be sub-divided. If the first part of the stanza was thus divided, the parts were called *pedes*, the musical theme or *oda* of the first *pes* being repeated for the second; the rest of the stanza was known as the *syrma* or *coda* and had a musical theme of its own. Conversely, the first part of the stanza might be indivisible, when it was called the *frons*, the divided parts of the second half being the *versus*; in this case, the *frons* had its own musical theme, as did the first *versus*, the theme of the first *versus* being repeated for the second. Or lastly, a stanza might consist of *pedes* and *versus*, one theme being used for the first *pes* and repeated for the second and similarly with the *versus*, the general principle being one of tripartition. The following examples[1] will make this clear.

I

Wiþ longyng y am lad,
On molde y waxe mad,
A maid marreþ me; } Pes.
Y grede, y grone, unglad,
For selden y am sad
Þat semly forte se. } Pes.

Diesis or Volta.

Leuedy, þou rewe me!
To rouþe þou hauest me rad,
Be bote of þat y bad,
My lyf is long on þe. } Syrma or Coda.

II

Jesu, for þi muchele miht,
Þou ȝef us of þi grace,
Þat we mowe dai and nyht
Þenken o þi face. } Frons.

Diesis or Volta.

In myn herte hit doþ me god,
When y þenke on jesu blod,
Þat ran doun bi ys syde, } Versus.
From is herte doun to is fot;
For ous he spradde is herte blod,
His wondes were so wyde. } Versus.

[1] Böddeker, W.L. III; G.L. X; W.L. VIII. Paul, *Grundriss der Germ. Phil.* II, p. 1058. Schipper, *Grundriss der Englischen Metrik*, p. 282.

III

Lenten ys come wiþ loue to toune, Wiþ blosmen and wiþ briddes roune, Þat al þis blisse bryngeþ ;	Pes.
Dayeseȝes in þis dales, Notes suete of nyhtegales, Uch foul song singeþ.	Pes.
	Diesis or Volta.
The þrestelcoe him þreteþ oo ; Away is huere wynter woo, When woderoue springeþ.	Versus.
Þis foules singeþ ferly fele, Ant wlyteþ on huere wynter wele, Þat al þe wode ryngeþ.	Versus.

The troubadours continued the principle of tripartition into the number of stanzas of which a poem consisted. This might be six, i.e. three equal groups, or seven or five, two equal and one unequal. These numbers of stanzas are not infrequent in Middle English lyrics.

Provençal poets used various forms of repetition as a means of uniting the separate stanzas of a poem: the last rime of one stanza became the first of the succeeding stanza, the extreme form of which device is found in the sestina. Middle English poets also repeated not a rime, but a word or words in the same way. Cases are "weping haueþ myn wonges wet" (Böddeker, p. 151) and some of Laurence Minot's poems.

Provençal lyrics usually concluded with a half-stanza, identical in form with the last half of the stanza in use, and containing an address, appeal or reference to the person for whom the poem was intended. This was known to the troubadours as the *tornada*, to northern French poets as the *envoi*.

Examples are found in Middle English lyrics, e.g.:

> y wole mone my song
> to wham þat hit ys on ylong[1].

The Middle English envoy does not often retain the stanza-form of the poem which it concludes. A typical instance is found in Chaucer's *Compleynte to his empty purse*.

The Provençal lyric stanza varies in length from two to forty-two lines; stanzas approaching the latter figure were, however, *tours de force*. New rimes in the same distribution might be employed for each stanza, or stanzas might be *unissonans*, i.e. the same set of rimes might be repeated in every stanza, as in the envoy to Chaucer's *Clerke's Tale* (in which the distribution of the rimes is nearly that of Bertran de Born's *Ges de disnar*, B.G. 80, 19); this, though common in Provençal, is unusual in Middle English. In stanzas from eight to sixteen lines in length, Middle English poets show strong resemblances to the troubadours in the disposition of their rimes, and in many cases full identity is apparent. (Stanza-forms of some complexity have been selected, as these provide better evidence than simple forms of Provençal influence upon stanza construction.) The form ababbcbc is used by the troubadours Albert de Sestaro, Guillem de Bergueda, Bertran Carbonel, Thomas, and in an anonymous

[1] Böddeker, p. 174.

pastorela[1]. It is the metre of the *Lament on the Death of Edward I*, and of the Anglo-Norman translation of that poem[2], of the *Lament on the Death of Edward III*[3] and of the refrain poem *Quia amore langueo*[4]. The *Song on the Execution of Sir Simon Fraser*[5] is in stanzas aabbcddc, an arrangement used by Raimon de Miraval[6]. The religious lyric *I syke when y singe*[7] is in the arrangement, ababccbccb, of a *tenso* by Rainaut de Pons[8]. "Jesu, for þi muchele miht[9]," coincides in rime-scheme (ababccdeed) with poems by Guiraut Riquier and Lanfranc Cigala[10]. "Lutel wot hit anymon[11]," ababbbcc (the last two lines a refrain), is a scheme used by Gausbert de Poicibot[12]. More numerous, as might be expected, are the modifications of certain typical forms. The arrangement aab ccb ddb eeb, etc., which was first elaborated by Marcabrun, as far as our knowledge goes, reappears in Middle English. The *Satire on the Consistory Courts*[13] has five stanzas aab ccb ddb eeb ff ggg f; the *Beauty of Ribbesdale*, aab ccb ddb eeb; "Lenten ys come wiþ loue to toune" and "In May hit murgeþ when hit dawes" have the same

[1] Maus, *Peire Cardinals Strophenbau*, Marburg, 1884, no. 306.
[2] Wright, *Political Songs*, Camden Society, 1839, p. 241, and Böddeker, p. 140.
[3] Wright, *Political Poems and Songs*, Rolls Series, 1, 216.
[4] Furnivall, *Political, Religious and Love Poems* (E. E. T. S. 15), p. 233.
[5] Böddeker, p. 126.
[6] Maus, no. 171.
[7] Böddeker, p. 210. The version in MS. Digby is slightly different.
[8] Maus, no. 342.
[9] Böddeker, p. 208.
[10] Maus, no. 377.
[11] Böddeker, p. 231.
[12] Maus, no. 300.
[13] Böddeker, pp. 109, 155, 164, 166.

rime arrangement. The type ababcdcd is seen in "weping haueþ myn wonges wet[1]" (abababab cdcd), which is nearly identical with a scheme used by two Italian troubadours, Dante da Majano and Paul Lanfranc de Pistoja[2]. Instances of this kind might easily be multiplied (see Appendix I).

Provençal lyric poetry included several *genres*, which are represented in Middle English. We propose to study these in succession and in sufficient detail to show similarities of thought and expression. The first is the *canso* or love poem, usually of five to seven stanzas with a *tornada* or envoy. A reference to the season of the year and its influence upon the poet's mood is a common beginning; in spring he may be cheerful or, if despondent, his melancholy will be increased by contrast with the brightness of nature: this was a favourite opening of Bernart de Ventadorn.

Lancan folhon bosc et jarric,
E·lh flors pareis e·lh verdura
Pels vergers et pels pratz
E·lh auzel, c'an estat enic,
Son gai desotz los folhatz...[3].

"When woods and bushes grow leafy, when flower and verdure appear in orchards and fields, and the birds, who have been idle hitherto, are cheerful under the foliage...."

Cant l'erba fresch' e·lh folha par
E la flors boton' el verjan,

[1] Böddeker, p. 151. The use of repetition to connect the stanzas and the reference to the "book of leuedes love," perhaps an imitation of the Provençal *Leys d'Amors*, are further points of contact with the troubadours.

[2] Maus, no. 239.

[3] B. de Ventadorn, ed. Appel, p. 140.

E · l rossinhols autet e clar
Leva sa votz e mou so chan...
Ai las! com mor de cossirar[1]!

"When the fresh grass and the leaf appear and the flower buds stud the orchard and the nightingale raises its voice high and clear and begins its song,...alas, how I die of longing."

Compare the first stanza of *Alysoun*:

Bytuene mersh and aueril
When spray biginneþ to springe,
Þe lutel foul haþ hire wyl
on hyre lud to synge.
Ich libbe in loue longinge
for semlokest of alle þinge;
He may me blisse bringe,
Icham in hire baundoun[2].

The resemblance is even closer in the case of an Anglo-Norman poet:

Quant le tens se renovele
E reverdoie cy bois,
Cist oysials sa pere apele
Cele cum a pris a choys;
Lur voil chanter sur mun peis...[3].

"When the fair weather is renewed and the woods again grow green, each bird calls its mate, the one whom it has chosen: then will I sing my grief."

Bernart de Ventadorn begins in almost identical terms:

[1] B. de Ventadorn, ed. Appel, p. 220.

[2] Böddeker, p. 147, note. "Verwandte Reimkonstruktionen finden sich auch bei den provenzalischen und altfranzösischen Lyrikern." The Provençal case is the *tenso* of Gaucelm Faidit, "N'Albert, eu sui en error," B.G. 157, 42, with rime-scheme ababbbbc.

[3] P. Meyer, *Les manuscrits français de Cambridge*, *Romania*, year 1886, p. 246.

Can lo boschatges es floritz
E vei lo tems renovelar,
E chascus auzels quer sa par
E · l rossinhols fai chans et critz,
D'un gran joi me creis tals oblitz
Que ves re mais no · m posc virar[1].

"When the wood is in flower and I see the weather grow fair again and each bird seeks its mate and the nightingale utters songs and calls, from a great delight such oblivion comes upon me that I cannot turn my mind to anything else."

So another Anglo-Norman of the 13th century:

En lo sesoun qe l'erbe poynt
E reverdist la matinee,
E sil oysel chauntent a poynt
En temps d'avryl, en la ramee,
Lores est ma dolur dublee
Que jeo sui en si dure poynt
Que jeo n'en ay de joie poynt,
Tant me greve la destinee[2].

"In the season when the grass appears, when the morn is again green-clad and the birds sing gaily in the branches, in April-time, then is my grief doubled, for I am in so hard a case, that I have no delight at all, so heavily does my fate oppress me."

The effects of unrequited love upon the poet are described in terms common to Provençal and

[1] B. de Ventadorn, ed. Appel, p. 226.

[2] P. Meyer, *Romania*, IV, p. 379. The poem continues in "derivative" rimes [part-partie], as they are called in the *Leys d'Amors* (I, 186). P. Meyer says: "c'est par une coincidence tout à fait fortuite qu'il se rencontre parmi les poésies de la comtesse de Die une pièce en rimes dérivatives et groupées selon l'ordre ababbaab (the rime-scheme of this piece), "Ab joi et ab joven m'apais" (*Parn. Occit.* p. 54).

Middle English lyrics. The poet sighs and groans, sheds tears, cannot sleep, and grows pale and thin.

> Nihtes when y wende and wake
> forþi myn wonges waxeþ won

says the author of *Alysoun*: so Peire Raimon de Toulouse declares:

> Per ma donna maigrisc et sec[1].

"For my lady I grow thin and pale."

> For hire loue in slep y slake,
> For hire loue al nyht ich wake,
> For hire loue mournyng y make
> More þen eny mon[2].

So Amanieu de Sescas:

> E la nueg, cant ieu cug dormir
> E·m soy colguatz per repauzar,
> non puesc, ans m'ave a levar
> per forsa d'amor en sezens[3].

"In the night, when I think to sleep and have laid me down to rest, I cannot; on the contrary, I sit up by constraint of love."

Or Raimon Jordan:

> Que, quant esguart la vostra gran valensa,
> Eu velh la noit, quan deuria durmir[4].

"When I consider your great worth, I am awake at night, when I should sleep."

If the lover were a bird, how easily could he approach his beloved!

> Ich wolde ich were a þrestelcok,
> A bounting oþer a lauerok,

[1] Ed. Anglade, p. 54. [2] Böddeker, p. 171.
[3] Appel, *Prov. Chrest.* no. 100, 1, 36.
[4] Ed. H. Kjellman, Upsala, 1922, p. 109.

aitant pauc co · l peissos
Viu ses l'aiga, viurai s'il platz mos dans
Midons ;

"As little as the fish lives without the water, shall I live, if my ruin pleases my lady";

or Arnaut de Maroill[1]:

Si com li peis an en l'aiga lor vida,
L'ai eu en joi e totz tems lai aurai.

"Even as the fishes have their life in the water, I have and ever shall have it in love's delight."

Under stress of suffering he feels himself sinking to an untimely death and beseeches his lady to have mercy on him:

& sent þou me þi sonde
Sone, er thou me slo[2];

or

Heo me wol to deþe bryng
Longe er my day[3].

So Guilhem Ademar:

Pres n'ai lo mal don cug qu'aurai la mort,
Si'n breu de temps no fai de que · m cofort[4];

"I have caught a sickness of which I think I shall have death, if in a short time she does not give me some comfort";

or Guilhem Montanhagol:

e s'ieu joi n'avia,
sai que non morria,
anz viuria gen pagatz.
Si non l'ai, morrai breumen,
qu'ieu l'am tan que · l cor m'estenh[5].

[1] B.G. 30, 22. Napolski, *ibid.* p. 105. [2] Böddeker, p. 149.
[3] *Ibid.* p. 162. [4] *Parn. Occ.* p. 258.
[5] Coulet, *Le troubadour G. M.*, Toulouse, 1898, p. 71.

"And if I should have delight of her I know that I should not die, on the contrary, I should live well content; if I have it not, I shall die soon, for I love her so much that my heart is breaking."

The lover is afraid to try his fortune, for fear of a refusal:

> Nys no fur so hot in helle
> al to mon,
> Þat loueþ derne ant darnout telle
> whet him ys on[1].

So Elias de Barjols:

> si · l tenc mon cor escondut
> qu'ieu no l'aus dir per temensa
> co · l sui francs e fis e leials[2];

"So I keep my heart hidden from her, for from fear I dare not tell her how true, faithful and loyal to her I am";

or Bernart de Ventadorn:

> Tan am midons e la tenh car.
> e tan la dopt'e la reblan
> c'anc de me no · lh auzei parlar.

"I love my lady so much and hold her so dear, and fear and reverence her so highly, that I never dare to speak to her of myself[3]."

The desired cure,

> A suete cos of þy mouþ mihte be my leche[4],

is prescribed in similar terms by Bernart de Ventadorn:

> Mas ab doutz sentir d'un baizar
> For' eu tost d'est mal resperitz[5].

[1] Böddeker, p. 162.
[2] Ed. Stronski, Toulouse, 1906, p. 17.
[3] Appel, p. 221. Cp. Raimon Jordan; Appel, *Prov. Ined.* p. 283.
[4] Böddeker, p. 174.
[5] Appel, p. 226.

"But by the sweet touch of a kiss, I should soon be recovered of this sickness."

A catalogue of the lady's beauties is a commonplace:

> Qui ve la fresca color
> de vos, bella, cui ador,
> e·ls uelhs vairs, e·ls cilhs delgatz[1].

"If one sees your fresh colour, fair one whom I adore, and the changing light of your eyes and their delicate lashes."

> Plus fresca que rosa ne lis.

"Fresher than rose or lily[2]."

> Roza de pascor
> Sembla de color
> E lis de blancor[3].

"She seems in colour as an Easter rose and a lily in whiteness."

> Hire rode is ase rose þat red is on rys,
> Wiþ lilye white leres lossum he is,

or

> Lylie-whyt hue is,
> Hire rode so rose on rys[4].

So an Anglo-Norman poet:

> Les euz veirs, nun pas volage,
> Beau neys avenant e dreit....
> . . . .
> Si les flurs de l'albespine
> Fuissent a roses assis,
> N'en ferunt colur plus fine
> Ke n'ad ma dame au cler vis;

[1] Coulet, *G. de Montanhagol*, p. 70.
[2] Cercamon. Bartsch, *Chr.* 48, 30.
[3] Peire Vidal, ed. Anglade, p. 121.
[4] Böddeker, pp. 145, 150.

Les espaules ben assis,
Poy le ney e la peitrine,
La char blanche plus ke cyne,
Par tut en porte le pris[1].

"She has sparkling eyes, not shifty, a pretty nose, fair and straight....If the mayflower were set upon the rose, they will make no finer colour than my bright-faced lady has; her shoulders are well set and her breast as snow (?), her flesh whiter than the swan: everywhere she bears away the prize."

Arnaut de Maroil's description is in similar terms:

Los vostres huels vairs e rizens,
E·l naz qu'es dreitz e be sezens[2],
La fassa fresca de colors,
Blanca, vermelha pus que flors,
Mento e gola e peitrina
Blanca, cum neus e flors d'espina[3].

"Your bright laughing eyes, your straight well-set nose, your fresh-complexioned face, white and redder than a flower, your chin, throat and breast whiter than snow or hawthorn flower."

Other coincidences of this nature are:

Ase sonnebem hire bleo ys briht,
in vche londe heo leomeþ liht[4].

venz enaissi trastot autra beutat,
cum lo soleils venz tot autra clardat[5].

"Thus she overcomes all other beauty, as the sun all other brightness."

hyre tyttes aren an vnder bis
as apples tuo of parays[4].

[1] P. Meyer, *Les manuscrits français de Cambridge*, *Romania*, 1886.
[2] "hire neose ys set as hit wel semeþ." Böddeker, p. 156.
[3] Raynouard, Choix III, p. 202. [4] Böddeker, pp. 155, 157.
[5] Raimbaut de Vaqueiras, Mahn, *Ged.* 76. Aimeric de Belenoi, M.G. 896.

Blanc peitz ab dura mamela[1].

"White bosom with firm breast."

Heo is rubie of riytfulnesse,
Heo is cristal of clannesse[2].

De robin ab cristaill
Sembla qe deus la fe[3].

"It seems that God made her of ruby and crystal."

The supreme happiness is thus expressed:

Heuene y tolde al his
Þat o nyht were hire gest[4];

or,

He myhte sayen þat crist hym seȝe
Þat myhte nyhtes neh hyre leȝe,
Heuene he heuede here[4].

So Peire Vidal:

E si ja vei qu'ensems ab mi · s despolh,
Melhs m'estara qu'al senhor d'Eissidolh[5];

or Raimbaut d'Aurenga:

Dieus prec, tan de mort m'escrima,
donna, e m'aja suffert,
tro q'ie · us embraz ses chamiza[6];

or Raimon Jordan, who considers the accomplishment of his desire as superior to the joys of Paradise:

Que tan la desir e volh,
Que, s'er' en coita de mort,
No queri' a Deu tan fort

[1] Peire Vidal, ed. Anglade, p. 48.
[2] Böddeker, p. 169.
[3] Aimeric de Belenoi, M.G. 896.
[4] Böddeker, pp. 150, 158.
[5] Ed. Anglade, p. 58.
[6] Appel, *Provenz. Inedita*, p. 265.

Que lai el seu paradis
M'aculhis
Com que · m des lezer
D'una noit ab lies jazer[1];

or Guilhem Ademar:

E per aisso tenc m'en per erebut,
E non enuei el mont nuil home nat,
si · m uol midon tenir uestit o nut
un ser lonc si en loc de muillerat[2];

or Raimbaut d'Aurenga:

Ben aurai, domna, grand honor
Si ja de vos m'es jutgada
Honransa, que sotz cobertor
Vos tenga nud' enbrassada[3].

The separation of lovers by daybreak, of which they are warned by a friend on guard, became the theme of a special lyric form in Provençal, the *alba*. The idea, of which *Romeo and Juliet* provides the best known example, is used in Chaucer's *Troilus and Criseyde* (III, 1465, 1702). The *alba* was a refrain song: there is an example in Middle English where the refrain

This gentill day dawes
And I must home gone,

is put into the mouth of a "comely queen" gathering roses in a "glorious garden[4]."

Among other Provençal inventions was a poem composed of contradictions or antitheses, known,

[1] Ed. Kjellman, p. 114.
[2] Suchier, *Denkmäler*, p. 321.
[3] Mahn, *Werke*, I, p. 77.
Cambridge Hist. English Lit. II, p. 384.

according to the *Leys d'Amors* as the *reversaris*[1]. The following is there given as an example:

Tu sentes greu freg en calor
E caut arden en gran frejor;
Le freytz te fay tot jorn suzar
E·l cautz glatir e tremolar:
Volontiers en dol totas horas
Rizes et en alegrier ploras.

"You feel grievous cold in heat and burning heat in great cold; cold makes you sweat all day and heat makes you shiver and shake; gladly you laugh at all times when in grief and in joy you weep."

The convenience of this device for describing a lover's distractions is obvious: we think at once of Charles d'Orléans, "Je meurs de soif auprès de la fontaine." An Anglo-Norman example is the following[2]:

Malade sui, de joie espris,
Tant suspire que ne repose;
Jeo ai mon quor en pensé mys,
E si enpens de nule chose;
Pover sui et de aver pleyn,
Et si ne sent ne mal ne bien;
De joie est tut mon quor certeyn;
Sages sui et si ne soi ren;
E jeo sui tant dolerouse
Plus jolifs homme n'est a nul jourz
Que moi ne ci ne aillors.

[1] Ed. Anglade, II, pp. 23 and 152.

[2] P. Meyer, *Romania*, VIII, p. 376 (I have made some obvious corrections). There are five stanzas, of which the first and last differ slightly from the rime-scheme of the other three: the scheme of the stanza quoted is Provençal (Maus, 390, less the last line).

Lydgate's *Compleynt* will serve for an English example[1]:

Myn wor[l]dely goddesse, & also
Myn Joye, myn helthe & ek myn wo,
Myn fulle trust & myn grevaunce,
Myn seknesse & myn hol plesaunce
Myn myrthe & ek myn maledye,
Myn langour & ek myn remedye,
Myn hertys rest & perturbaunce,
Myn syghynge & myn suffysaunce,
Myn comfort & countrycyoun,
Myn dol, myn consolacioun,
Myn laughynge & myn wepynge ek,
And cause whi that I am sek,
Myn though[t] a day, myn wach a nyght,
. . . .
My holsum drem whan that I slepe,
But whanne I wake, thanne I wepe;
Myn hertys Joye, where ȝe gon,
And I in langeur ly alon,
Nothyr fully quik nor ded
But al amasid in myn hed.

Many of the features most characteristic of the Provençal *canso* are wanting in the Middle English lyric. There is no technical vocabulary of love: equivalents for joi, cortesia, solatz, etc., do not appear. The attempts at psychological explanations of love's beginning and progress are not made. Absent also are the ideas of love as a service which improves those who loyally bear its burden, and the pains of which are in reality a supreme delight. The English lyric is more direct in expression and more genuine in sentiment than the troubadour

[1] *Continuation of the Temple of Glas*, E. E. T. S. No. IX, 1891, p. 495.

poems, and borrowed from them, mediately or immediately, nothing more than its stanza-form and a few more or less conventional thoughts of the kind above detailed. Thus it does not attempt the lengthy and elaborate similes which certain troubadours affected. Coincidences in this respect are to be found:

> me were leuere kepe hire come,
> þen beon pope & ryde in rome
> styþe upon stede[1].

So Bertran de Born says that his lady in accepting him has made him richer than a king:

> Et a · m dat mais de ricor
> que s'era reis de Palerna[2].

Similarly, two geographical points are stated, within which the paragon is unrivalled:

> One of hem ich herie best
> from Irlond in to ynde[3].

So Uc d'Albi:

> quar sa valors sai qu'es tan granda
> que dels Portz entro en Yrlanda
> pot, si · l plai, triar els melhors[4].

"For I know that her worth is so great that one can, if he will, choose from the Pyrenees to Ireland,"

without finding her equal.

The Anglo-Norman poet compares his heart to a burning torch:

> Tot ensi va de mun cor
> Cum d'une torche eslumee[5].

[1] Böddeker, p. 157. [2] Ed. Stimming, p. 90.
[3] Böddeker, p. 166. [4] Appel, *Prov. Inedita*, p. 156.
[5] P. Meyer, *Romania*, VIII.

So Peire Raimon de Tolosa:

> Atressi com la candela
> Que se meteissa destrui[1].

"Even as the candle which destroys itself" to give light to others, so I sing in spite of my woes.

Allusions to the evil work of backbiters and slanderers and warnings to the lady against them also form a parallel between southern French and Middle English erotic poetry; the latter adopted the continental terms and englished them as losynger and trichour[2] in preference to the Anglo-Saxon (swyke). But here again no detailed analysis is made of these adverse influences.

More of these parallelisms are given in the Appendix. As has been already said, many of them are to be found in the *trouvères* of northern France and no doubt reached England by that route. It may also be assumed that many of them are obvious commonplaces which would occur to any lyric poet. On the other hand, when we consider the close political and commercial relations existing between England and southern France, it is reasonable to assume that some influence was directly exerted by Provençal lyric poetry: and however trivial many points of comparison may appear, it must be admitted that their cumulative effect is considerable.

The secular lyric was adapted by English poets at an early date for religious purposes: the efforts of Thomas of Bayeux, archbishop of York, to this

[1] Ed. Anglade, p. 25.   [2] Böddeker, pp. 137, 166.

end have been already mentioned (p. 11). The same stanza constructions are found, the same conventional opening with a reference to the seasons: winter arouses the reflection that "we all do fade as a leaf" and that the joys of this world are transitory. Spring rouses desire to sing the joys of divine love. The pastoral form of lyric is utilised for a meditation upon the five joys of the Virgin. Many parallel passages may be found, e.g. the healing power of the Virgin:

Betere is hire medycyn,
þen eny mede or eny wyn;
hire erbes smulleþ suete;
from Catenas in to Dyuelyn
nis þer no leche so fyn
oure serewes to bete[1].

So Peire de Corbiac:

Domna, metges e mezina,
lectoaris et enguens,
los nafratz de mort guirens;

"Lady, physician and medicine, lectuary and unguent, healing the death-stricken[2]";

or Guiraut Riquier:

Et etz restaurans mezina,
Fons de vera pietat,
Als fallens
Etz guirens
D'amara
Mort[3].

Such coincidences as these are, however, no proof of Provençal influence in this particular case, for

[1] Böddeker, p. 214. [2] Bartsch, *Prov. Chrest.* 234.
[3] Mahn, *Werke*, IV, p. 16.

the reason that both Provençal and English may be indebted to a common source. In the *Tractat dels noms de la mayre de Dieu*[1], a poem which introduces a large number of appellations of the Virgin, nearly every title applied to the Virgin by English poets is to be found, including that of the healer (d'omes hyest medecina). While troubadours may have invented some of these, the Church was undoubtedly the original source of most of them. We might, for instance, regard the hymn "Gabriel from evene King" as written upon a troubadour stanza-form, since the rime-scheme is remarkably similar to a Provençal type, if we did not possess the Latin original, "Angelus ad virginem," the hymn of the Clerk of Oxford in Chaucer's *Miller's Tale.*

The *sirventes* among the troubadours was a lyric poem similar in form to the *canso*, but differing from it in content, in that it excluded love and sentiment and dealt with personal, political or ethical issues. The two last-named forms are well represented in Middle English lyric poetry. The "Song against the King of Almaigne" composed shortly after the battle of Lewes, the song on the execution of Sir Simon Fraser in 1306 (which has a Provençal rime-scheme) are true political *sirventes.* Under this heading must also be classed the *planh*, a lament on the death of some patron or king, which was a common form of tribute paid by troubadours to the memory of great men. Instances

[1] *Daurel et Beton*, P. Meyer, *Anciens Textes français*, Paris, 1880, p. cv.

are the lament on the death of Edward I, of which both an Anglo-Norman and an English version exist (the rime-scheme is Provençal ababbcbc, Maus, no. 306), and the lament on Simon de Montfort. The laudatory phrases (flur de pris), the references to the power of death and the sorrow which it brings recall troubadour language on the same theme.

Poems dealing with the evils of the age, the oppression of the nobles, the decay of morals, the immorality of churchmen and the like also occur in *sirventes* form. The *Satire on the Consistory Courts* is in highly elaborate form, and is composed of five 18-line stanzas; the first 12 lines are almost identical in the disposition of the rimes with a form used by Raimbaut d'Aurenga[1]. The *Song of the Husbandman* is in stanzas two lines shorter, but otherwise identical with a stanza-form used by Dante da Majano[2], the final verse of one stanza being connected with the first verse of the next by the repetition of a leading word. The poem on the earthquake of 1382[3] has a rime-scheme used by five troubadours[4]. The subject-matter of these poems is obviously suggested by local or national circumstances and coincidences of thought between Provençal and English writers are due, where they exist, to similarity of conditions and not to conscious imitation. There is, for instance, a certain resemblance between Peire Cardinal's invectives against

[1] Maus, 185. [2] Maus, 239.
[3] Wright, *Political Poems*, Rolls Series, I, p. 253.
[4] Maus, 306.

the Roman Church and those produced in England, but the resemblance is due to the fact that ecclesiastical abuses were everywhere similar in character. The Anglo-Norman satire, *Le Ordre de Bel-Eyse*[1], discusses the foundation of a new order which shall combine the characteristic vices of the existing orders, and upbraids the gluttony of the Black Monks, and the neglect of fasting by the Canonici, whereas Peire Cardinal[2] accuses the latter of usury: both agree upon the pride and ostentation of the Hospitallers.

The Anglo-Norman poem by Edward II[3] written in captivity after his deposition bears strong traces of Provençal influence. The rime-scheme abababab is used by two troubadours (Maus, 211); the poem opens with the conventional reference to the season of the year and ends with an envoy; it is addressed to a lady, whose name is concealed under a *senhal*: the stanzas are *encadenadas*, i.e. a catchword in the last line of one stanza is repeated in the first line of the next.

Crusade songs, which were produced by several famous troubadours, also fall under this head. I can find no example in English and only one in Anglo-Norman (in J. Bédier, *Les Chansons de Croisade*, Paris, 1909, p. 67), which reproduces the exhortations usual in all these songs.

The *tenso* was among the troubadours a discussion

[1] Wright, *Pol. Songs*, Camden Misc. p. 141.

[2] M.G. 977. Peire Cardinal is more easily compared with the Anglo-Latin satirical poets. See Vossler, *Sitzungsberichte der königl. bayerischen Akademie*, 1916, München, p. 138.

[3] P. Studer, *Modern Language Review*, XVI, p. 34.

in verse between two interlocutors, sometimes three, who replied to one another in alternate stanzas, defending or attacking a thesis laid down in the opening stanza. A *tenso* between a lover and his lady could be conducted on these lines and assertion and reply could be given in alternate lines, instead of in alternate stanzas. "My death y loue, my lyf ich hate[1]" is a dialogue in alternate stanzas: Aimeric de Pegulhan[2] has one in alternate lines. A further development reduced the conversation to stichomuthia, as in the following[3]:

"I do complayn and [can] find no release."
"Yee, do ye so? I pray you, tel me how."
"My lady lyst not my paynys to redres."
"Say ye soth?" "Yee, I make god a vowe."

"Who ys your lady?" "I put case you."
"Who, I? nay, be sure, yt ys not soo."
"In fayth, ye be." "Why do ye swere now?"
"For, in good fayth, I love you and no moo."

"No mo but me?" "No, so sayd I."
"May I you trust?" "Yee, I make you sure."
"I fere nay." "Yes, I shall tel you why."
"Tell on, let's here." "Ye have my hart in cure."

"Your hart? nay." "Yes, wythout mesure,
I do you love." "I pray you, say not so."
"In feyth I do." "May I of you be sure?"
"Yee, in good fayth." "Then am I yours allsoo."

The "back-chat" in the following from Peire

[1] Böddeker, p. 172. Of a similar type is "In a fryht as y con fere fremede," Böddeker, p. 158.

[2] Bartsch, *Prov. Chrest.* col. 175.

[3] Ritson, *Ancient Songs and Ballads*, p. 162.

Rogier[1] moves more rapidly, but is of the same kind.

Ailas!—Que · t plang?—Laissi · m morir.
—Que as?—Am.—E trop.—Ieu, oc tan
Qu'en muer.—Mors?—Oc.—Non potz guerir?
—Ieu, no.—E cum?—Tan suy iratz.
—De que?—De lieys don suy aissos.
—Sofra.—No · m val.—Clama · l merces.
—Si · m fatz.—No y as pro?—Pauc.—No · t pes,
Si en tras mal.—Noqua o fas de lieys.

Cosselh n'ai.—Qual?—Vuelh m'en partir.
—Non far.—Si farai.—Quers ton dan.
—Qu'en puesc al?—Vols t'en ben jauzir?
—Oc, mout.—Crei me.—Era diguatz.
—Sias humils, francs, larcs e pros.
—Si · m fai mal?—Suefr'en patz.—Sui pres.
—Tu?—Oc.—Si amar vols, e si · m cres,
Aissi poiras jauzir de lieys.

"Alas! Why complain? Let me die. What is the matter? I am in love. And deeply. Yea, so that I die of it. Art dying? Yea. Canst not be cured? Not I. And why? So stricken am I. Of whom? Of her for whom I care. Endure. Avails me not. Cry her for mercy. That do I. Advantageth thee not? Little. Grieve not, if thou bear ill of it. Never do I from her. I have counsel. What? I will depart from her. Do not so. I will. You seek your loss. What can I else? Wilt thou have joy of her? Yea, much. Believe me. Say on. Be humble, frank, liberal and worthy. If she does me ill? Bear it in peace. Ready am I. Art thou? Yea. If thou wilt love and believest me, thus shalt thou be able to have joy of her[2]."

[1] Mahn, *Werke*, I, p. 124. Other examples are Albert (de Malaspina?), Bertoni, *Trovatori d'Italia*, p. 469. Arnaut Ploges, *Parn. Occ.* p. 357. Elias Cairel, ed. Jäschke, Berlin, 1921, p. 195 (the troubadour here converses with himself). Elias de Barjols, ed. Stronski, Toulouse, 1906, p. 57.

[2] Compare also Giraut de Bornelh, *Ailas, com mor!* B.G. 242, 3.

This is an extreme and burlesque form of the *estrif*, as it was known in northern France. The conversations of Mr Alfred Jingle or of Mary Ann and Mrs Simmons in *Le Roi des Montagnes* were almost equally poetical.

The *tenso* form was also used in England as a wholly imaginative setting, as in the following case which is put in the form of a dream:

> Volez escuter un deduit
> Ke jeo oy cestre (*sic*) autre nuit
>   Tut en cochaunt
> Entre trés duz fin' Amur
> Et un prodome de grant valur
>   Issi disant.
> Amor, amor, u estes vous?
> —Certes, sire, en poi de leus,
>   Car jeo ne os.
> —Pur quei nen osez estre veu,
> Vous ki estes si bien conu
>   Et de bon los[1]?

Amur laments that he has been driven away by enemies such as Coveitise and recounts his former achievements.

The *tenso* form was used, as was the form of the secular lyric, by Middle English poets, for religious purposes. The *Dispute between Mary and the Cross* has much resemblance to a Provençal *tenso* on the same subject (though no metrical affinity)[2]; the *Disputison bytwene a Christenemon and a Jew*,

[1] Ed. J. Vising, Göteborg, 1905. *La plainte d'Amour*: *Romania*, XIII, 507, XV, 292, XXIX, 4, XXXII, 73.

[2] P. Meyer, *Daurel et Beton*, p. lxxiii, who gives the Latin poem by Philippe de Grève which may have suggested the idea. The rime-scheme of the English poem is nearly that of Maus, 242.

the *Dialogue between the Virgin and Christ on the Cross* (Stond wel, moder, under rode), the *Debate between the Heart and the Eye*, the *Debate between the Body and the Soul* are of this type. Of the last named a Provençal version is extant and there are versions in most European vernaculars; it is possible that a Latin poem ascribed to Walter Mapes was the original of these[1]. *The Owl and the Nightingale*, the first of many similar animal debates, is a further development of the same idea: one of the interlocutors in the Provençal *tenso* might be an animal or even an inanimate object (a horse, swallow and cloak thus appear); but there is no case in which both disputants belong to the animal kingdom.

The pastoral (*pastorela*), which appears to have originated in the south of France, was a poem relating the meeting of a knight and a shepherdess and the conversation between them. Our own nursery rime, "Where are you going, my pretty maid?" is a pastoral in full form. The conventional opening in Provençal was "l'autrier," "the other day," which is retained in the religious lyric, "As y me rod þis ender day[2]." Secular lyrics of this kind begin with the same formula: such are "Now springs the spray[3]" and one as yet apparently unpublished[4]:

[1] Wright, *Latin poems of Walter Mapes*, Camden Society, p. 95.

[2] Böddeker, p. 218.

[3] This poem (Skeat, *Modern Language Review*, vol. IV, p. 236), which is a true pastoral, starts with the same line as the religious poem. There is no need to suppose, as Skeat hints, that one was imitated from the other: the opening is identical, because it was conventional.

[4] Camb. Univ. Library Ff. v. 48, f. 119 a; the MS. is damp-stained and in parts illegible.

As I me went this andyrs day
Fast on my way makyng my mone,
On a mery mornyng of May
Thurgh Huntley Banke myself alone.

The poet Thomas lies under a tree to listen to the birds, when the inevitable lady appears and the usual conversation proceeds. The pastoral naturally became a *chanson d'aventure*, relating how the poet went into the country or to church, what persons he met and what experiences he had with them. The *Fair Maid of Ribbesdale*, the *Meeting in the Wood*[1], and several other lyrics are in this setting. The pastoral proper is concerned with the conversation of a knight and a shepherdess or village maiden, to whom he offers his love and by whom he is accepted or refused.

English religious poetry of this period has its counterpart in Provençal, so far as subject-matter is concerned. Hymns to the Virgin, the Seven Joys of the Virgin, the Gospel of Nicodemus, the Childhood of Christ, the Virgin's Complaint[2], the History of the Rood-Tree, the Dispute between Mary and the Cross are, for instance, subjects common to both literatures. The quotation of parallel passages would prove nothing in this case, as Latin originals were usually the source whence similarity of thought or expression proceeded. Northern French was also a source common to both literatures: the English poem on the fifteen signs before the Day of Judgement belongs to a group

[1] Böddeker, pp. 155, 158.

[2] *Plaintes de la Vierge en Anglo-Français*, F. J. Tanquerey, Paris, 1921.

of versions based on a French original from which the Provençal version was translated[1]. An exception is *Ypotis, the Wise Child who conversed with the Emperor Hadrian*: the editor[2] of the Provençal text regards the English version as derived from it and not from a French intermediary.

Eine Tatsache die gegen diese Annahme Bedenken erwecken könnte, ist mir nicht bekannt. Wer sich scheuen sollte den englischen Text unmittelbar auf einen provenzalischen zurückzuführen, müsste noch eine weitre, gänzlich verlorne französische Übersetzung zwischen beiden einschieben; mir selbst scheint das nicht notwendig.

These observations also apply to theological and didactic literature. Treatises on doctrine, dietetics, the training and conduct of the young (stans puer ad mensam) occur in both literatures, and similarities are due to a common source of origin and not to borrowing by English writers from Provençal. So, again, in the case of epic poetry: Fierabras figures both in English and Provençal; the Provençal *Daurel et Beton* has affinities with the story of Sir Beues of Hamtoun: in either case, the original is to be found in northern France.

Thomas, the author of the *Roman de Tristan*, was probably an Englishman and certainly lived and wrote in England between 1155 and 1170. "Er

[1] MS. B 11, 24, Trin. Coll. Camb., pub. E.E.T.S. no. 24 (1867), p. 118. The Provençal in Suchier, *Denkmäler*, p. 156. For literature on the subject, see Suchier's notes, and P. Meyer, *Daurel et Beton*, p. xcvii.

[2] *Das prov. Gespräch des Kaisers Hadrian mit dem klugen Kinde Epitus*, W. Suchier, Marburg, 1906, p. 53.

[3] *Geschichte der Französischen Litteratur* (1900), p. 131. See Bédier, *Le roman de Tristan*, Paris, 1895, vol. II, pp. 47 and 57.

dürfte Gedichte der Troubadours gekannt haben, denn einzelne seiner Stellen klingen an diese an," says Suchier. Conversely, references to the Tristan legend occur in Provençal literature, but there is nothing to show that they refer to the version of Thomas rather than to any one of the other versions of the story in circulation. Thomas is of the school of Chrétien de Troyes; he gave a courtly and chivalrous colouring to a legend originally savage and brutal, because he lived in a chivalrous atmosphere and wrote for a courtly public. He may have known troubadour poems, as Suchier says, but involuntary reminiscences and not conscious imitations of them are the most that his *Tristan* can show.

The type of allegorical literature made fashionable by the *Roman de la Rose*, in which virtues and vices are personified and some stately building, a palace or temple, is made the scene of the action, is also found in Provençal. The *Chastel d'Amors*[1], a fragment of 180 lines, describes the Castle of Love, its circuit walls, the arrangement of its interior, etc. The French poem from which Bishop Grosteste translated his *Castel of Love*, is a religious application of this allegory, the Virgin appearing as the castle of love, defended by four forts—the cardinal virtues, three baileys, her maidenhood, chastity and wedding—with a well inside, the spring of Grace and so forth. More important is the *Cour d'Amour*[2], also incomplete, with 1730 lines.

[1] A. Thomas, *Annales du Midi*, 1889.

[2] L. Constans, *Les manuscrits provençaux de Cheltenham*, Paris, 1882, p. 66.

The unknown author calls his poem a "romanz," intended to teach the true method of love. "Fin' Amors" is discovered holding her court on the summit of Parnassus with her servants about her.

El temps qe · l roissignol faz nausa,
Que de nueit ni de zor no pausa
Desotz la fuella de cantar,
Pel bel temps que vei refrescar,
Aven que Fin'Amors parlet
Ab sos baros en son rescet,
En son del puei de Parnasus;
Zoi e Solasz foron laisus,
E Ardimens e Cortezia,
Qe de flors l'en zonchon la via;
Bon Esperancha e Paors
Li porton de denant las flors;
D'autra part, Larguesza e Donneis
Lo meton en un leit d'orfreis;
Celars e Dousa Conpania
Geton desus idesa floria.
Lo cortes pueih, de l'autra part,
Del fuoch d'amor relusz e · s art:
E d'aqui mout tota la joza
Qu'Amors per mei lo mond'envoza.
E d'autra part son las floretas,
Las ruosas e las violetas,
Qi trameton lor gran douszor
Denant lo leit de Fin'Amor.
E d'autra part ha cent pulsellas,
Q'anc negus hom non vi plus bellas;
E chascuna ha son amador,
E son vestu d'una color,
E · s baison e · s braisson soven,
E mantenon pretz e joven;
E totz temps han aital desdug,
Ad aital gen vai be, so cug,

E d'autra part hac un ombrage,
On hac maint bel auzel saulvatge,
Que canton la nueit e lo zor
Voltas e lais de gran dousor,
Ez el mei loc ac un castel,
Q'anc negus om non vi plus bel,
Que non ha una peira el mur
Non luisza con d'aur o d'azur.

"In the time that the nightingale lifts up her voice and ceases not to sing night and day beneath the leaf, in the fair time that I see bringing freshness, it happens that Pure Love speaks with her barons in her retreat, on the summit of the hill of Parnassus: Joy and Solace were there and Ardour and Courtesy who strewed the way with flowers; Good Hope and Fear carry flowers before her; on the other side, Largesse and Gallantry lay her on a couch of orfrey; Secrecy and Sweet Companionship likewise cast flowers thereon. The court hill, moreover, shines and glows with the fire of love and thence proceeds all the joy which Love sends through the world. There also are flowers, roses and violets which spread their great fragrances before the couch of Pure Love. There too are a hundred maidens, more beautiful were never seen, and each has her lover, and both are dressed in one colour and often they kiss and embrace and are ever young and gallant, and ever they have such delight; such people are in good case, I ween. There is moreover a wood where are many wild birds which sing night and day trills and lays of great sweetness and in the midst of the place is a castle—never was one more beautiful seen—for the wall has not a stone which does not shine with gold or blue."

There is a considerable resemblance between this passage and those stanzas of Boccaccio's *Teseide* which Chaucer translated or imitated in his *Parlement of Foules*[1]. The *Chastel d'Amors*, it should

[1] Skeat, *Minor poems of Chaucer*, p. lxii, quotes the stanzas.

be said, has been thought to be of Italian origin and this *Cour d'Amour* was certainly copied by an Italian scribe. In any case it was anterior to the *Roman de la Rose* and if it did not set, may have done something to popularise the idea of Venus and her Court of Love (which, of course, has no connection with the legendary Courts of Love fathered upon troubadour society by Nostradamus and André le Chapelain). The idea itself may go back as far as Ovid.

In conclusion, the facts may be thus summarised. We find Middle English poets displaying high technical skill in the use of stanza-forms which are surprisingly complex, when we consider the poverty of their language in rime. We find that the structure of the stanza and the disposition of the rimes are, in many cases, identical with forms used by Provençal poets. We further observe that the poetical *genres* in vogue are similar to those affected by the troubadours, and that the English treatment of them displays similarities of thought and expression which, if sometimes trivial in themselves, are too numerous in their totality to be explained as due to chance coincidence. We have noted the close commercial and political relations of England with southern France, the interest shown by the troubadours in English politics and the fact that at least two leading troubadours are known to have been in England. These points alone would entitle us to infer that the influence of troubadour poetry upon the English lyric was considerable.

On the other hand, the spirit of the Middle

English lyric is not that of the troubadours; if forms were borrowed, another and more vigorous life was breathed into them. We have to take into account the further facts that the public likely to be interested in poetry from the 12th to the 15th century was largely bilingual and conversant as well with Anglo-French as with their own tongue; northern French lyric poetry, which this public undoubtedly read or heard, had at that time been strongly influenced by Provençal, and produced poems which were often close imitations and sometimes almost translations of troubadour originals. Hence the unmistakable traces of Provençal influence may have reached this country as well from northern as from southern France. The merchant of Corbie or Arras may have sung imitations of troubadour lyrics in his London *Puy*; but the *joglar* of southern France may also have found the members of this confraternity an appreciative audience. There is no evidence available which will enable us to decide between these alternatives or to distinguish the relative strength of two simultaneous streams of influence. None the less, it is clear that English lyric poetry owes a great debt to the troubadours. Their influence may not have been so immediate or so profound as it was upon the literatures of Italy, Spain or Germany. But its traces are unmistakable and cannot be neglected; any history, for instance, of English stanza-forms is obliged to take Provençal lyric poetry as its starting point or to remain incomplete.

APPENDIX I

The following is a list of the rime-schemes in Middle English and Old Provençal which correspond precisely. It should be remembered that a large number of complicated rime-schemes in the two literatures differ only in some one rime; these and stanzas with less than six lines are not mentioned here. Numbers preceded by M. refer to the table in Maus, *Peire Cardinals Strophenbau*, Marburg, 1884; numbers preceded by W. refer to pages in Wells, *A manual of the writings in Middle English*, Yale University Press, 1916.

aaaaabab.	M. 22.	Hayl, Mari, hic am sori. W. 534.
aaaabb.	M. 29.	Patris Sapiencia. W. 359.
aaaabcb.	M. 38.	Song against the king of Almayne. W. 211.
aaabab.	M. 50.	No more willi wiked be. W. 500.
aaabcb.	M. 75.	Ase y me rod this ender day. W. 536.
aaabcccb.	M. 77.	Ichot a burde. W. 493.
aabbcc.	M. 150.	Influence of Planets. W. 437.
aabbccd.	M. 158.	How the good wife taught her daughter. W. 380.
aabbcddc.	M. 171.	Song on the execution of Simon Fraser. W. 212.
aabccb.	M. 181.	Proverbs of Hendyng. W. 377. Sayings of St Bernard. W. 389. Quite common.
aabccbddb.	M. 184.	Jesu Crist, heouene Kyng. W. 522.
ababaababa.	M. 205.	On hire is al mi lif. W. 534.
abababab.	M. 211.	Will and wit. W. 383. Song on Death. W. 391. Psalms. W. 404, and several other examples.
ababbba.	M. 292.	Mirie it is. W. 491. Now springes the sprai. W. 497.
ababbbcc.	M. 300.	Lutel wot hit anymon. W. 503.
ababbcbc.	M. 306.	Psalms. W. 404. Elegy on Edward I and III. W. 213, 217. Vernon Simeon lyrics, ten times. W. 508. Quite common.
ababbcc.	M. 308.	I knowlech to God. W. 524.
ababcbcb.	M. 331.	Song on the times. W. 213.
ababccbccb.	M. 342.	Hi sike al wan hi singe. W. 518.
ababccdeed.	M. 377.	Jesu, for thy muchele miht. W. 522.
ababcdcd.	M. 383.	Crist, give us grace. W. 513.
ababcded.	M. 408.	As Thou for holy Churche. W. 526.

APPENDIX II

Several poems have been collected here which illustrate more particularly Provençal influences and are not readily accessible to many readers.

I

Lambeth MS. 306, fol. 137 vo., E.E.T.S. 15, p. 71.

That pasaunt Goodnes, the Rote of all vertve,
which Rotide is in youre femynete,
whos stepes glade to Ensue
ys eueri woman in their degre!
And sethe that ye are floure of bewte,
Constreyned y am, maugre myn hede,
hartely to loue youre womanhede.

2

Your sade, Demewre, appert goueronance
Of eliquens prengnavnt sauns coloure,
So it Renyth in my Rememberaunce
that dayly, nyghtly, tyde, tyme and owre,
hit is my will to purches youre fauoure,
whiche, wilde to Crist I myght atteyn,
As ye of all floures Are my Souerayn.

3

Whan Reste And slepe y shulde haue noxiall,
As Requereth bothe nature and kynde,
than trobled are my wittes all,
so sodeynly Renyth in my mynde
your grete bewte! me thynketh than y fynde
you as gripyng in myn armes twey;
Bute whan y wake, ye are away.

4

Entirmet this with woo And gladnes,
bothe Joye and sorowe in woo memorall,
for than me thynkithe y see your likenes;
hit is nat so, it is fantasticall;
the whiche my herte with þe swarde mortall
that nothinge is, saue uery Dethe,
my wette is thynne, so schortithe my breth.

5

Nowe, lady myn, in whome Vertus Alle
ar Joined and also comprehendide,
as ye of al women y call moste principall,
lette my gref in youre herte be entenderde,
And also my veri treue loue Rememberde,
And, for my treve loue, ayene me to loue,
As welethe neture, and god that setithe Above.

6

Go litill bill, with all humblis,
vnto my lady, of womenhede þe floure,
and saie hire howe newe troiles lithe in distreȝ
All onely for hire sake and in mortall langoure;
And if sche wot nat whoo it is, bute stonde in erore,
Say it is hire olde louer þat loueth hire so trewe,
hire louynge alone, not schanging for no newe.

This poem is of somewhat late date (about 1450) but is interesting for the number of troubadour commonplaces which it contains; in particular, it repeats ideas from the love letter of Folquet de Romans. The rime-scheme, ababbcc, was used by Aimeric de Pegulhan, Folquet de Marseille, Pons de Capduelh (Maus, 308).

Stanza 1.

Qu'ensenhamen e beautatz,
Cortezia e gen parlars,
Gent aculhirs et honrars
Joyos, ab franca semblanza,
Vos fan sobr'autras honransa.
Arnaut de Marueil. M.W. I, p. 171.

Qu'ab bel semblan, franc e cortes,
avez mon cor lassat e pres,
tan que d'al re no pueis pensar
Mais de vos servir et onrar.
Folquet de Romans, ed. Zenker, p. 72, 21–30.

"For wit and beauty, good breeding and speech, kindly greeting and glad attentions with frank bearing, bring you honour above other women."

"For with gracious, frank and kindly bearing you have captured my heart, so that I can think of nothing but of serving and honouring you."

Stanza 3.

D'ir' e d'esmay, domna, m'avetz estort
pel bon coven on ai tot mon conort,
que, quant esgart la vostra gran valensa,
eu velh la noit quan deuria dormir,
e pens soven si pot esdevenir
que vos m'aiatz tan granda benvolensa.

Raimon Jordan. Kjellman, p. 109.

Que la nueit, quan soi endurmiz,
s'en vai a vos mos esperiz;
donna, ar ai eu tan de ben
que quan resvelh e m'en soven,
per pauc no·m volh los olhz crebar
quar s'entremetton del velhar;
e vauc vos per lo leich cerchan,
e quan no·us trob, reman ploran;
qu'eu volria toz temps dormir,
qu'en sonjan vos pogues tenir.

Folquet de Romans, ed. Zenker, p. 72, 21–30.

Soven m'aven la nueg, quan sui colgatz,
Qu'ieu sui ab vos per semblan en durmen;
Adoncs estauc en tan ric jauzimen,
Qu'ieu non volgra ja esser rissidatz,
Tan cum dures aquel plazenz pensatz;
E quan m'esvelh, cug murir deziran,
Per qu'ieu volgra aissi dormir tot l'an.

Arnaut de Marueil. M.W. I, p. 165.

"From rage and fear, lady, you have delivered me by means of the kind promise wherein I have all my comfort so that, when I consider your great worth, I am awake at night when I should be sleeping and often consider if it could be that your kindness should be so great."

"For at night, when I am asleep, my spirit goes forth to you; lady, then such happiness is mine that when I wake and memory returns, I scarce believe my eyes, for they struggle to wake; and I search through the bed for you, and when I find you not, I abide weeping; for I would like to sleep ever so that I might hold you in my dream."

"Often it happens to me at night, when I am in bed, that I am with you in seeming as I sleep: then am I in such rich delight that I could wish never to be awakened, so long as that pleasing thought endures. And when I wake, I almost die of longing, wherefore I could wish thus to sleep all the year."

Stanza 4.

Mos cors no·s pot per ren partir de vos,
Ans en durmen me vir mantas sazos,
Qu'ieu joc e ri ab vos, e·n sui jauzire;
Pueis, quan reissit, vey e conosc e sen
Que res non es, torn en plorar lo rire.

Arnaut de Marueil. M.W. I, p. 165.

"My heart can by no means depart from you: on the contrary in sleep it often seems to me that I am jesting and laughing with you and I rejoice thereat: then when I wake, I see, know and feel that it is naught, and laughter turns to tears."

Stanza 5.

Dona, genser qu'anc fos de nullas gens,
E la melher de totas las melhors,
Per vos morrai, so·m ditz ades paors,
Si no·us en pren merces e chauzimens:
Bona domna, aiatz en sovinensa
Al cor, e ja no m'en fassatz parvensa,
Tro conoscatz que ben sia sazos
Que·m n'eschaia qualque ricz guizardos.

Arnaut de Marueil. M.W. I, p. 150.

"Lady, the noblest that ever was of any, and the best of all the best, for you I shall die, so my fear tells me ever, if you do not have mercy and pity on me: good lady, have it to heart in memory and make no pretence of it to me, until you know that the time has come for some rich reward to fall to my lot."

Stanza 6.

Ten, chanson, drita via
A la bella on que sia,
E di li q'ie·l faza saber
Qu'autra non voill qe sia
De mon cors garentia.

Peirol. M.W. II, p. 14.

"Song, take a straight road to the fair one[1], wherever she may be and tell her that I assure her that I will have no other to be the keeper of my heart."

[1] The theme "Go, little book" of the conclusion of Chaucer's *Troilus* is common enough and no doubt originated with Ovid, *Tristia* I, 1–3, *Ex Ponto* IV, 5 and elsewhere.

II

Cambridge University Library, MS. DD. 10. 31, fol. 5 vo. P. Meyer, *Romania*, xv, p. 253.

1\. Quant le tens se renovele
E reverdoie cy bois,
Cist oysials sa pere apele
Cele cum a pris a choys;
Lur voil chanter sur mun peis 5
D'une dame gent e bele,
Sur trestutes tourturele.
Ben fuyst al plus grant reis
Ke unkes seit en see n'en deis,
Tant est noble juvencele; 10
Mès ver moi tut tens revele,
Si me respunt en gabeis.

2\. Tant ad noble contenance
Cele pur ki faz cest chant,
Sage diz e poi parlance, 15
Duz regard e bel semblant.
Mut est simple e poi riant,
Ben se contient cum d'enfance.
Tant vus di, tut sanz vantance,
Loinz ne près n'ad per vivant; 20
Sire serreit sun amant
Si ele l'amast par fiance.
Mès jo n'ai nul'esperance
Cument la puis amer tant.

3\. Deu ! tant est de bonté pleine 25
Ma dame al cors lunge e gent,
E de parole certeine
Beaus respunt [a] tute gent.
Bon mestre a ki ben aprent,
Kar curtesie la meine, 30
Franchise al cuer dreit l'aseine,
Largesce sun cors i prent;
Meint hom pur lui joie enprent,
Tant la trove sage e seyne;
Mès jo'n ai trop mal estreine 35
Sanz l'angoisse a gref turment.

4 Sa beauté ne puis descrire,
Tant ay ver lui bon'amur.
Deu de gloir[e] reis e sire
Kant li fist si bele honur 40
Ke de bealté tient la flur,
Nuls ne poet contredire.
Pur li meynent doel e ire;
Mut de gent par grant folur,
Pur reprender lur vigur, 45
Chescun d'els en li se myre,
Mès j'en sofre gref martire,
Tant me destraint ma dolur.

5. Tut le plus de s'estature
Orra ki le voet savoir; 50
Mut ad beau chef sanz triffure,
Large frunt e surciz noir;
Ja n'esparnerai le voir;
Tant ad bele chevelure,
Menue la recercelure, 55
Tut en resplent un manoir.
Ki porreit sun gre avoir
Mal n'avroit fors k'enveisure,
Mès jo, cheitif sanz mesure,
Ai perdu sen e savoir. 60

6. Plus i a en tel visage,
Ja l'orrez si nul me creit,
Les euz veirs, nun pas volage,
Remuanz a bel espleit,
Beau neys avenant e dreit, 65
Meine buche sanz utrage,
Mentun petit cum d'ymage,
Lung le col, le quir estreit.
Ne puis savoir ke me deit
Quant ne chevis mun message, 70
Mès jo en ai la vive rage,
Tant sui mis en fort destreit.

7. Si les flurs d[e l']albespine
Fuissent a roses assis,
N'en ferunt colur plus fine 75
Ke n'ad ma dame au cler vis;

40 MS. la. 50 MS. Ore a. 55 MS. retercelure.
62 MS. treit. 63 MS. nunt.

Les espaules ben assis,
Poy le ney e la peitrine,
La char blanche plus ke cyne,
Par tut en porte le pris; 80
Dunt suy si forment suspris,
Ne sa[i] k'amur me destine,
Mès ceo feis me runt l'eschine,
Si m'esta de mal en pis.

8. Coment ke ço feis me greve, 85
Quant le savra ne me chaut,
Tant m'en est la mort plus sueve
Kar amur en mey ne faut,
De tut l'el coment k'il aut.
Ore dirai parole breve; 90
Ki trop enprent mal escheve;
Fol apris[e] ren ne vaut.
Si ne me preisse al plus halt
Ne me preisasse une feve,
Mès cis mals le quer me creve; 95
Ben sai ke frai un fous saut.

9. Ore deit ben chescun entendre
Cum amur est cher tresor;
Ki la pert sa joie est mendre,
Kar meuz li vausit estre mort. 100
Jo sui si mortelement mors
Ke le quer m'estuit [tut] fendre.
Puis k'ele ne voet pité prendre,
Ben crei ke men seit le tort,
Valer ne me poet nul jur, 105
Puis ke mort me voet esteyndre,
Mès a Deu voil l'alme rendre
E a ma dame mun cors.

The rime-scheme is ababbaabbaab (to which the first stanza does not strictly conform). The first eight rimes form a combination used by ten troubadours (Maus, 280). The last two lines of each stanza form a half refrain, introduced by *mes*, and stating the poet's hopeless case. The poem follows the usual course of a troubadour *canso*: it opens with a reference to the spring time as a cause of

87 MS. sentue.

inspiration, announces the attractions of the lady's disposition and temperament, catalogues her physical charms and contemplates death as a conclusion to hopelessness.

l. 1. The usual troubadour commonplace: see p. 106.

l. 7. *tourturele.* Peire Vidal, Anglade, no. xvi, 40, "et es columba ses fiel." Middle English used "tortle" in the same sense: Böddeker, p. 161.

ll. 13 ff.

> Qu'ensenhamen e beautatz,
> Cortezia e gen parlars,
> Gent aculhirs et honrars
> Joyos, ab franca semblanza,
> Vos fan sobr'autras honransa.
>
> Arnaut de Marueil. M.W. I, p. 171.

"For wisdom and beauty, courtesy and good speech, kindly greeting and ready honour, with frank bearing, exalt you above others."

l. 29. Amors, as well as Cortesia, is referred to as a schoolmaster by troubadours.

> Que gen m'a duoich de las artz de s'escola.
>
> Arnaut Daniel. Canello, p. 116.

"For he has well initiated me into the artifices of his school."

l. 37. See pp. 113–114 for the description of personal attractions.

l. 46. The idea of the lady as a mirror in which others can discover their good or bad qualities is a troubadour commonplace, and passed from Provençal into several literatures.

> Qu'e·l falhimen d'autrui tanh qu'om se mir
> Per so qu'om gart se mezeis de falhir.
>
> Folquet de Marselha. Stronski, no. xiv, 40.

This, Stronski points out, is Terence, *Ad.* 415, "Inspicere tamquam in speculum in vitas omnium Jubeo atque ex aliis sumere exemplum tibi." So Bertran de Born, Stimming, ix, 29, "chascus si mir el jove rei engles." Giraut de Bornelh, *Los apleitz.*

Chaucer, *Man of Law's Tale*, 166; Shakespeare, *Antony and Cleopatra*, Act v, Sc. i; *Julius Caesar*, Act I, Sc. ii;

Calderón, *La Cisma de Inglaterra*, I, iv; Schiller, *Wallenstein*, I, 7, line 468, "Ein rechter Kerl sich darin spiegeln mag," are more modern instances.

l. 78. P. Meyer suggests "piz levé."

l. 91. "Qui tot vol tener tot pert," Folquet de Romans. Zenker, VI, 30.

l. 94. The nut, onion and other similar objects are used by troubadours as standards of infinitesimal value in this way.

l. 104. Arnaut de Marueil throws the blame on the lady. M. W. I, p. 165:

> Per so, en dreit d'amor, vos er peccatz
> Del mal qu'eu ai; e per vos muer aman,
> Que non fora, se non valgues aitan.

"Wherefore, in love's law, you are to blame for the ill that I have: and for you I die of love, which would not be, were you not of such great worth."

III

Cambridge University Library, MS. DD. 10. 31 (f. 3 a). P. Meyer, *Romania*, XV, p. 248.

> 1. Lung tens ay de quer amé,
> Celé l'ay d'estrange gyse.
> S'en ai grant tort e peché
> Ke ma dame n'ay tramise
> L'amur k'en lui ay assise 5
> De fin quer sanz fauseté,
> Dunt la serf en lealté
> E serveray sanz feintyse.
> Du celer faz grant mesprise;
> Si m'eb confès a sun gré; 10
> En chantant, ma verité
> Faz saver a sa franchise.
>
> 2. Dame, quant primes vus vi,
> Tant futes de bealté fine
> De tut mun quer vus seysi, 15
> Vus en avez la racine;

Mès vus k'estes enterine
de cors e de quoer ausy,
N'en seustes mot ne demi;
S'en ay trop dure trayne. 20
Meuz vousisse mort sovine
Ke vivre longes ensy;
Ben le saches tut de fy,
Ja sanz vus n'avray mescine.

3. Tut ensi va de mun cors 25
Cum d'une torche eslumé[e];
La char se destruit dehors,
Si n'esteynt point ma pensé[e].
Jo vus [aim], dame honuré[e]
En ki remeint mes tresors, 30
Mès jo n'en ai nul confort;
Cele est ma destinée
Coment en ay grant hastée
Mein e seir, sanz nul deport.
De vos beals euz m'avez mors; 35
Si vus plet, treben me greye.

4. L'unicorn, quant veit dormir,
Se baundone a la pucele;
Ne prent garde de morir
Quant uns armé l'anbouele. 40
Ensi m'est, m'amie bele;
Voz bunté voil obeyr,
Voz ferté me voet ferir
Du mal dunt la mort m'apele,
Si n'os dire me querele 45
Ne mun penser descovrir.
Cum poet vos buntez suffrir
Ke voz ferté tant revele?

5. Pus ke n'os od vus parler,
La mort m'est trop ben venue, 50
Mès si vus pleseit abreger
La peyne k'issi me tue,
Mut vus serreit grant value
Si me pussez alleger
D'un sul beau respuns, dunt 55
M'avrez la vie rendue.

Soviengez vus ent, ma drue,
Ke sanz vus ne pus durer;
Si vus puys ben aficher,
Kar d'autre ne quer ayue. 60

Rime-scheme as No. II (on which see note) but without refrain. The poet has been restrained by fear from declaring his passion (a common *motif*, see p. 112) but feels that he must now speak or die.

En joy ai mon esper,
Fin cor e ferm voler.
Arnaut de Marueil. M.W. I, p. 167.

l. 6 *fin*. A regular epithet in troubadour lyrics.

l. 13. Quant en premer la vi, me plac aitan,
Que de mon cor retener non puec ges:
Totz fo ab leis et ancaras i es.
Peirol. M.W. II, p. 28.

"When first I saw her, she pleased me so that I could not keep her from my heart: it was all hers and is so yet."

l. 18. The play of words on *cors* and *cor* is common in troubadours: a number of passages are collected by De Lollis, *Sordello*, p. 279. It is also common in Chrétien de Troyes.

l. 24. A common description of the Virgin in religious poetry is "mezina dels peccadors." The metaphor is used by Guillem de Berguedan, "So c'az amor es veraia messina" (M. G. I, 167, 2), though not in such direct reference to the lady as here.

l. 25–7. See p. 120.

l. 35. See p. 110.

ll. 37 ff. P. Meyer points out that the comparison of the lover with the unicorn is used by the King of Navarre in *Ausi com l'unicorne sui* (Scheler, *Trouvères belges*, I, 144). I am unable to find any similar use in Provençal. (See, however, *Annales du Midi*, vol. XXIX, p. 269, n. 1, where a suggestion is made that this simile may have been borrowed from Provençal.)

IV

P. Meyer, *Romania*, IV, p. 374. MS. 1285, Ashmolean collection, Bodleian, Oxford. The interlinear variants may be author's corrections or readings from another text of the same piece.

1. De ma dame vuil chanter
 Ke tant est bele et bloie.
Se m'i peüsse aseürer
 Trestut sen seroie;
De lui leaument amer
 Quer e cors metroie;
Ja autre n'aurai en penser
 Fors tant que tut sen soie.
Trop s'esluine; las! pur quei?
 Aura ele ja merci de mei?

2. Duce dame, de mei grever
 Ne seez pa[s] si aprise
 Pur quei estes si aprise,
Quant deu tut en vus amer
 Ai m'entente mise?
Mes par vostre deboneirté
E vus sul tant par esluiner
 Rendez m'en servise
 Rendez mun service.
Deus! ki me purra reheitier
 se n'est
 Quant tele est ta devise!
Trop s'esluine, si s'en veit:
 a
 Li deu d'amur tot le renveit!

 La joie
3. Deus! kar seüst ore la bloie
 valance
 Ke trai pur s'esluinance.
Je qui ke de meuz auroie
 Sa bone vuilance,
Kar en li, si Deu me voie,
 Tut'est ma fiance.

De lui me duinst uncore joie
Cil ce (*sic*) tuz avance.
Trop s'esluine mun confort
E ma joie e mun deport.

4. Duze dame, dès ore vus pri
Pur cil ke dit est sire,
Ke deu mal aiez merci
Ke tant mun quer empire:
Mien n'est il pas! tu l'as seisi,
Si en seez le mire!
Deu! tut ai a li faili,
Trop ot od mei martire.
Trop s'esluinne de cest païs
Las! ke frai, tant sui pensis!

5. Au definer de ma chançun,
Oez me desestance,
Kar en vus est la garisun
Deu mal ke au quer me lance;
Ne quer garir se par vus nun,
Tant n'ei au quer pesance.
Pur Deu vus pri e sein Simun
Ke me facez legance.
Trop s'esluinne tut le desir
Dunt je quer au quer joïr.

Rime-scheme abababab cc, the last two lines forming a half refrain. This scheme was used by the troubadours Peire Cardinal, Sordello, Guiraut Riquier and Bertran d'Alamanon (Maus, 222) and all except the last mentioned used a refrain. There is a distinct similarity between this Anglo-Norman poem and Sordello's (De Lollis, xxx): the subject-matter of both is the despair of a lover whose lady will not look kindly upon him: cp. with the opening lines, Sordello 7–9:

Si·lh qu'es donna de plazensa
Chantarai, sitot d'amor
Muer, quar l'am tant ses falhensa.

"If I sing of her who is lady of delight, though I die of love, for I love her so loyally."

With lines 11–14 compare Sordello 33–35:

Ai, per que·m fai ta mal traire?
Qu'ilh sap be de que m'es gen
Qu'el sieu pretz dir e retraire.

"Ah, why does she lay such ill upon me, for she well knows how I delight in telling and recounting her worth?"

The refrain repeats Sordello's ilha·m vol de si lunhar (l. 26), "she wishes to keep me at a distance." Line 35 is Sordello's

Elha·m pot far o desfaire,
Cum lo sieu....

"She may make or mar me as I am hers."

There are, however, differences which make it impossible to speak of direct imitation. Sordello does not address the lady directly: his refrain lays stress on deprivation of sight of his beloved: his resignation to his fate is more complete. The Anglo-Norman contains ideas which are not found in Sordello's poem; such are the play on *quer* and *cors* (l. 6), the request that the lady shall be the healer of his pain (ll. 36 and 42) though these are troubadour commonplaces (see notes to No. III).

V

Pembroke College, Cambridge, MS. no. 113. A. T. Baker, *Revue des Langues Romanes*, LI, p. 40 (year 1908). *Chansons Satiriques et Bachiques*, Jeanroy et Långfors, Paris, 1921, no. XXIII.

1. El tens d'iver, quant vei palir,
l'erbe pur la freidure
e les menuz oisels tapir
en la ramee oscure,
a grant dolur suvent suspir, 5
tant vei eisir
amur de sa nature:

5 MS. sument.

la bele a qui joe pens e tir,
senz rien merir,
me gref a desmesure. 10
En icele esperance,
me delite ma peine
ki les amanz avance
d'aveir goie certeine.

2. Cele ki tant aim e desir, 15
m'ocit senz forfaiture,
quant si sultif me lait languir,
qu'ele ne m'aseüre;
ker tut sui sons a sun pleisir,
senz repentir, 20
si ke d'altre n'ai cure;
purquant si m'est gref cest martir,
tuz tens suffrir
et vivre en aventure.
En icele....

3. Joe vei un usage tenir 25
as dames senz dreiture
dunt eles funt vite perir
amur veraie e pure
e les amanz sovent marrir,
e revertir 30
en grant desconfiture.
ceste me fait a poi murir,
e pur ceo m'ir
qu'el m'est si fere e dure.
En icele....

4. Entre dous verz pot l'em veïr 35
ke la terce est maüre,
mais unc ne poi une coisir,
ki ne m'ait esté sure;
purquant si ne m'em pus partir,
n'aillurs guenchir, 40
ain sofre ci...[ure].
cist las ne set ke devenir
ne u fuir,
ceo li pluvist e jure.
En icele....

24 MS. en.
41 le MS. semble avoir *ci*; on ne peut lire que la partie supérieure de l'f.

5. Li custumer d'eles traïr — 45
   trovent large pasture,
mès a mei ki ne sai mentir
   fu d'amur l'ambleüre
amer e preier e fallir;
      me fait fremir — 50
   e me tient en rancure;
kar unques ne me poi saisir,
      ceo puis plevir,
   d'anel ne de ceinture.
   En icele....

6. Laial amant deivent haïr — 55
   feinte amur e tafure,
kar a ceos ki'n deivent goïr
   n'at mester cuverture;
en merveille deit l'om tenir
      de faus cuvrir — 60
   cumment nus quers l'endure:
pur ceo vei duz amur languir
      e esbaïr
   sur tote creature.
   En icele....

This poem is written in a 13th century hand with musical notation on a blank page in a MS. of Juvenal and Persius. The rime-scheme ababaababaab was used by the troubadour Guiraut d'Espanha (Maus, 204). The refrain is similar in idea to a refrain used by the same troubadour (Appel, *Prov. Ined.* p. 163):

> e ia guerir del mal d'amor no vuelh,
> ans m'abellis mays, on pus fort m'en duelh.

"I do not wish to be cured of the pain of love, on the contrary, the more I suffer, the greater my delight."

The opening is conventional and the reference to the ring in stanza 5 alludes to a troubadour custom. The complaint in stanza 3 is somewhat characteristic of Guilhem de Saint Leidier, as is the disappointed tone of the whole poem.

> Quar costum'es que domna sia dura;
> . . . .

Blasmar deu hom un usatge que y cor,
Que fan domnas, qu'ieu non lur tene a sen.
(Mahn, *Werke*, II, pp. 41 and 54.)

The first lines of stanza 4 allude, as the editors point out, to a proverb quoted by Mistral in modern Provençal:

Entre dos verdo uno maduro, (*Trésor*, madur)

the sense being that pleasures and pains alternate in life, and the poet has never been able to choose any but the latter. Bertran de Born used the terms in a similar sense:

Quan n'ac trach lo vert e·l madur.
(Stimming, no. 12, l. 61.)

"When he has taken from them the green and the ripe," i.e. everything.

VI

St John's College, Cambridge, MS. 138, f. 125, fragment of a song-book bound into the MS. The rime-scheme is ababccdeed, used by Guiraut Riquier and Lanfranc Cigala (Maus, 377). The conventional opening has been sufficiently illustrated.

En averil al tens delits
ke oysels funt chanter si gay,
quant rechet li tens jolifs
en contre la seysun de may,
et dames et damaysels
sunt plus quentes et plus beles,
de vis bloy culure,
et checun en sa manere
de amer fet semblant et chere,
cum cil ke est en amure,
Lors mi sovient bon amur
et bele dame sanz mentir,
ke jeo soye nuit et jur
de qor pensifs....

The Rotruenge.

This was a lyrical form which originated in northern France and made its way southward, and in this case alone does troubadour lyric poetry appear to have borrowed from the north. The passages proving this statement are given in P. Meyer's article in *Romania*, XIX, pp. 37 ff. Convention regarded French as the correct language for the rotruenge: the well-known passage in Raimon Vidal's *Razos de trobar* says, "La parladura francescha val mais et es plus avinens a far romanz, retronxas e pastorellas." Hence perhaps the scarcity of the Provençal *retroncha*, though examples are found. Probably for this reason Gaucelm Faidit's *can vei reverdir los jardis* was originally written in French, as Crescini argues[1]. The same may be true of Richard's captivity song[2]. The rotruenge is nothing more than a *canso* with a refrain and it is not easy to understand why northern French should have been thought more suitable than Provençal for this special form. It was known under this name in England. In the Chronicle of Jordan Fantosme (Rolls Series, III, line 1310) when the Scotch abandon the siege of Wark in 1174

> N'i aveit pas reprueces ne dite vilanie
> Mes suns e rotruenges et regrettent amie.

The derivation of the term is far from clear. P. Meyer (*loc. cit.*) rejected *retro* (on the very adequate ground that it would become *reire* in Provençal and *riere* in French) and preferred to connect the term with *rote*, a stringed instrument, but he was unable to account for -ruenge. The *Leys d'Amors* seems to prefer *retro*: "alcun altre apelo retroncha...per so quar retroncho, so es retorno soen un mot, o dos, o tot un verset." (Anglade, *Bibl. Méridionale*, II, p. 31.) If a form "retroientia" can be assumed, it might have produced retroensa: *retro* in isolation would have developed otherwise.

[1] *Atti e memorie della R. Acc. di Padova*, XXVI, p. 63. Kolien, *Dichtungen der Trobadors*, Halle, 1919, p. 161, speaks of it as a "Kanzone," and appears to consider that its original form was in Provençal. See also K. Lewent, *Zeits. rom. Phil.* XL, 2, year 1919, p. 226.

[2] See note to p. 57.

VII

Rotruenge.

British Museum, MS. Addit. 16,559, last fly-sheet but one. P. Meyer, in *Romania*, XIX, p. 103.

1. Quant primes me quintey de amors
A luy me donay a tuz jors,
Mès unkes n'oy si dolur noyn
E peyne.
Va ester ke dundens va, etc.

2. Je em la plus bele du pais;
Kaunt je m'ene pens si sui jolifs.
Je l'em plus ke ne fit Paris
Heleyne.
Ester, etc.

3. Les chevoys li lusent cumme fil de or;
Ele ad le col lung & gros,
Si ne y pert frunce ne os
Ne veyne.

4. Ele ad les oyz vers e rianz,
Les denz menu rengé devant,
Buche vermayle fete cume teint
En greyne.

5. Ele ad beu braz pur acoler,
Ele ad duz cors pur deporter;
Un mort purra resuciter
Sa alayne.

6. Kaunt ele git entre mes bras
E je le acole par grant solaz,
Lor vint le jor que nus depart
A payne.

7. Ore voil ma dame reprover
Ke ele me dedeyne amer.
Plus est gente ke un espervir
K'en reclayme.

1 Corr. m'acointai. 3 noyn for non.

8. Ma dame, a Deu vus kemaund.
Seez tuz jors leal amaunt;
Nul ne pout estre vaylaunt
Si n'eyme.

Ester ke dundele, etc.

The refrain is obscure and seems to be given in an incomplete form, even in the first stanza. Date, second half of the 13th century. Rimes of stanza 7 show that the author was English. The rime-scheme aaab (Maus, 41) is used by Guillaume IX and other troubadours. The reference to Paris and Helen in stanza 2 is used by Arnaut Daniel (Canello, p. 98); Lamberte de Bonanel:

Q'ie·us am plus senes mesura
qe no fetz Paris Elena.
Herrig, *Archiv*, 33, p. 451.

For the catalogue of the lady's beauties, see p. 113. In stanza 7 *reclamer* was the technical term for recalling the hawk, as Daude de Pradas explains in his treatise on falconry. It is used metaphorically by Jaufre Rudel:

E non puosc trobar meizina
si non vau al sieu reclam.

"And I can find no relief, if I do not return to her call." (Stimming, p. 45.)

But I can find no precise parallel to this metaphor. Peire Vidal compares the process of wooing with that of hawk-taming (Anglade, no. xliii). The hyperbole in stanza 5 appears in a Spanish *Razón de Amor* which is obviously of French origin, "mas ell olor que d'i yxia | a omne muerto ressucitarya" in reference to a flower-bed. (*Revue Hispanique*, XIII, p. 610.) I know of no other instance. The concluding sentiment is a troubadour commonplace.

VIII

Emmanuel College, MS. 106, f. 11 b. Copy in Dr James' catalogue, p. 169.

Mon queor me dist que doi amer,
Mes ieo ne sai ou empler
Amour que tut temps puet durer;
  Pur ceo sui en langour.
Qui mei savera enseigner 5
  Ou ficherai m'amour?

Si ieo desire biens et richesces,
Ieo vei les riches en granz destresces,
Au departir doil et tristez;
  Pur ceo sui en langour. 10
Ieo querrai ioie plus adrez
  Ou ficherai m'amour.

Si ieo desire estre sage,
Pruz et bien de haute parage,
Ieo vei que tut ceo faut en age; 15
  Pur ceo sui en langour.
Ieo querrai ioie en autre age
  Ou ficherai m'amour.

Si ieo desire mours et vertutz
Pur quei ieo sui preise de tutz 20
Aschun defautz i ad desuz;
  Pur ceo sui en langour.
Ieo querrai ioie pure lasuz
  Ou ficherai m'amour.

Si ieo desire estre honurable, 25
Honur de ceste secle n'est que fable
Ffaus et faint et deceivable;
  Pur ceo sui en langour.
Ieo querrai ioie plus estable
  Ou ficherai m'amour. 30

Ore entendetz dount ieo m'affie;
Ieo voiz queraunt oue la Marie,

4 sui] su. 5 savera] sauerai. 8 granz] grant. 19 vertutz] uertuez.
20 sui] su. 24 ficherai] fichera. 31 m'affie] me affie.

Douz Ihesu fontaine de vie,
  Qui garish de langour,
En qui soule ioie est acomplie; 35
  La ficherai m'amour. Amen.

The rime-scheme aaabab is interesting, as it is used three times by Guillaume IX of Poitiers, the first of the troubadours, and also by Bernard Marti and Marcabrun (Maus, 50). None of these uses a refrain, as here, for which this primitive stanza-form is especially suitable. The theme of the poem, that the things of this world are not proper objects of love, has been used by many poets: of troubadours, Guiraut Riquier used it more than once.

Quar no viu ben en amor
Hom, si non es agradans
A la maire, qu'es pregans
So filh, nostre redemptor.
(Mahn, *Werke*, IV, p. 65.)

IX

Caius College, Cambridge, MS. 11, first fly-leaf. P. Meyer, *Romania*, XXXVIII, p. 439.

E! Dame Jolive,
Mun quer sauns faucer
Met en vostre balaie,
Qe ne say vos per.

1. Sovent mi vais cumpleinaunt
E a mun qer dolur grant
  De ma maladie,
Pur quey tut fin lel amaunt
Deivunt aver joie grant 5
  Qe itel mal me mestrie.
Si souvent me agrie
Li duz mal de amer
Qe par sa seignurie
Me couvent chaunter. 10
  E! Dame etc.

6 itel] P. M.'s corr. for *il tal*.

2. Jeo eyme ou quer desiraunt
De munde la plus plesaunt
E la meus preysie;
Sages est e ben parlaunt;
En honur si attendaunt 15
En mund nasqui mie.
Ne say qe jeo en die,
Meis, a dreit parler,
C'est la meus enseignie
Qe hom pusse trover. 20

3. Ben say qe fel enquisaunt
Me sunt tut ade[s] nuisant
Vers nostre partie.
Dame a gent cors avenaunt,
Pur Deu, ne creez pas taunt 25
Felun plen de envie.
Si tres male vie
Lur voile Deus doner,
Qe ans pussent mie
Moy vers vus coureser. 30

4. Unkes nuls qe se fit amaunt
Ne mit sa peine si graunt
De servir sa amie
Cum jeo ay fet tut mun vivaunt
De entere sa duz semblant 35
Pur esgayer ma vie.
Si l'ehusse en ma baylie
Par sa volunté,
De ma grant maladie
Serroie garé. 40
E! Dame Jolive.

This poem is written in a 14th century English hand on a fly-leaf of a text of Justinian written in Italy in the 14th century and ornamented in England, according to Dr James. P. Meyer regarded it as consisting of four stanzas of six lines, alternating with four stanzas of four lines,

19 C'est] se. 20 corr. puist.
29 P. M. read *Qe il ne p. m. Trop vers.*
36 MS. esgger, with abbreviation mark on first g. P. M. read *elgger* and suggested *aleger*.

the latter being identical with the refrain. There seems no sufficient reason for adopting so unusual an arrangement, nor does the MS. suggest it. The poem seems to me to consist of four *coblas unisonans*, to use the Provençal term: (the change of rime in ll. 38 and 40 is not unusual in Anglo-Norman verse:) the rime-scheme is aabaabbcbc, a variant of Maus 306. The refrain, which is placed in full at the beginning, is noted at the end of the first and last stanzas and no doubt the scribe assumed that it would be taken for granted at the end of the other two stanzas.

The references to the joy of love-sickness, the *duz mal de amer* in stanza 1, to the lady's high qualities in stanza 2, to the slanderer in stanza 3 and to the pleasure of service and the remedy for suffering in stanza 4 are all troubadour commonplaces which have been sufficiently illustrated elsewhere.

INDEX

CAMBRIDGE: PRINTED BY THE SYNDICS OF THE PRESS
AT THE UNIVERSITY PRESS

INDEX

CAMBRIDGE: PRINTED BY THE SYNDICS OF THE PRESS
AT THE UNIVERSITY PRESS